PILGRIMAGE OF THE SOUL

Thresholds to the Mystery

Sally M. O'Neil & Suzanne K Seaton

ii

Library of Congress Control Number: 2004098137

ISBN: 0-9658844-2-2

Cover image: A three dimensionsl "spiral" fractal image derived from the "Julia set" in The Science book, Cassell and Co., London, 2001.

Published by Soaring Eagle Publishing
PO Box 578
Freeland, WA 98249-9501

Printed In the U.S.A. by
Morris Publishing
3212 East Highway 30
Kearney, NE 68847
1 800-650 7888

ENDORSEMENTS

"Finding one's authentic self has always been a journey with few guides and even fewer maps to chart the way. The irony is that since we are each unique, we are the only ones who will ever know this territory intimately. So we are destined to be our own guides and our own mapmakers. It is not an easy task! Recognizing this, the authors have provided exactly what we need to chart our unique paths. Both authors clearly know of what they speak, for they have both discovered the joy and freedom of self-realization in their own lives." *Hal Zina Bennett, Ph.D., author of* Write From the Heart *and more than 30 successful books.*

"This is an excellent treatment of a subject in which "Baby Boomers" and GenXers" have been showing keen interest. *Pilgrimage of the Soul* will offer readers who want to grow and to gain a sense of integrity. You have assembled a rich store of illustrations from experience, your own and others', which not only helped me to grasp the point but injected a sense of hope that I can attain authentic selfhood.""In the way this book is designed, it would make a very good textbook for classes in spiritual formation or spirituality taught in seminaries or colleges. I would like to use it in an 'Introduction to Spirituality' which I teach each fall semester, for instance, and a colleague who conducts required classes in 'Spiritual Formation' would also like to use it. I would also envision considerable usage of your book among church formation classes or possibly Sunday School or other classes of young adults. In the church of which I'm a member, for example, we have done book studies of books such as *Pilgrimage of the Soul* in which we focused on a chapter each week. It might also be adopted as a textbook in spiritual direction programs such as *Sursum, Corda*, a spiritual direction program of the Episcopal Diocese of South Carolina, or in spiritual formation programs such as the Academy for

Spiritual Formation." *E. Glenn Hinson, Th.D., Ph.D., Professor Emeritus, Baptist Theological Seminary at Richmond.*

"This book is a pure delight to read and absorb. I absolutely loved it. Although written by two persons, it emerges as one voice expressing the profound universal truths for which we all instinctively yearn. While exploring the distinctions between illusions and truth, ego and spirit, self and soul, the book also offers spiritual practices that can lead to places of oneness and transformation. Although it will be particularly helpful to pastors, counselors and spiritual leaders, I think it is a book for anyone who yearns for a spiritually authentic life, regardless of profession or age." *The Reverend Dr. Rodney R. Romney, Pastor Emeritus of Seattle First Baptist Church. Author of* Wilderness Spirituality. *Boston: Element Books, 1999*

"*Pilgrimage of the Soul* weaves story, psychology and spirituality into a journey of greater authenticity and fulfillment. Suzanne Seaton and Sally O'Neil take the struggles of the work world seriously and offer creative suggestions and wise counsel to people overly busy yet feeling disappointedly empty." *The Reverend Larry Peacock, United Methodist pastor in Malibu, CA, spiritual director and retreat leader. He is the author of* Heart and Soul – a guide to spiritual formation in the local church. *Nashville: Upper Room Books, 1992.*

"*Pilgrimage of the Soul i*s a very insightful and practical help to almost any reader who is conscious of his or her personal being and its growth and development. Beyond that, it should challenge those who are not yet self-consciously aware but who have hit the walls of life that stop us and demand that we rethink everything, to become introspective about their own journeys. Confused as we are at those points in our lives, this book is a very practical help in enabling us to find ourselves, discern and name some of the problems, and feel less lonely and desperate as we find ourselves in the company of others who are walking along the path of self-discovery from ego to oneness.

The frequent use of quotations and experiences are a very effective device for bringing the psychological concepts home to individual cases with which we can identify. It also kept the book interesting. It is a very inviting read and once started should draw the reader to go on to the end." *Hazelyn McComas – Milwaukee, WI Faculty member of the Milwaukee Theological Institute.*

"*Pilgrimage of the Soul* is a unique blend of psychological metaphors, suggestions for the spiritual life, and probing questions that would benefit most readers to consider. To me, the self-reflections sections are the heart of the book where the ideas discussed are put into practice. It is an original book that should be helpful to a wide variety of people." *The Reverend Anne Broyles, Retired United Methodist minister. Writer and retreat leader. uthor of* Journaling: A Spiritual Journey, *and* Growing Together in Love: God Known Through Family Life, *Nashville: Upper Room Books, 1993.*

"This articulate book would be helpful to all spiritual seekers, both beginners and those more advanced. The quality of *Pilgrimage of the Soul* would make it an excellent choice for some of our spirituality courses in our Masters program in spirituality here at the School of Theology and Ministry at Seattle University." *Dr. Marianne LaBarre, Director, Pastoral Leadership Program, Seattle University, Seattle, WA*

"*Pilgrimage of the Soul* describes the movement from a conventional, up-the-ladder kind of life, into the crisis. It provides people a way to understand what is happening to them when everything they wanted isn't enough, and that becomes the beginning for something more. A helpful illustration of the human Spirit emerging into fullness of life. Using uncomplicated language, the authors depict the dynamics of spiritual transformation." *The Reverend Jerry Haas, United Methodist Minister, Executive Director of the Two year Academy for Spiritual Formation, Nashville, TN.*

TABLE OF CONTENTS

INTRODUCTION

CONVERSATION

Angel: . . . *What I have to tell you now is neither good nor bad. It's just necessary.*

Unborn*: All right, what is it?*

Angel: *It's that sometime while you are waiting to be born, you start forgetting. By the time you're actually born, you will have forgotten everything. . . everything we've talked about. You won't remember me or ever having been here.*

Unborn*: I won't remember anything? Nothing? None of the secrets? Oh, that sounds bad to me. In fact, that sounds terrible.*

Angel: *But it really isn't. You see, if you did remember, you wouldn't really be entirely human. If you remembered, you wouldn't take your life "there" seriously. You might think it didn't matter. And it does. It matters urgently. So you forget "here." Oh, from time to time in the years after you're born, you'll have certain feelings that you won't quite understand: certain longings, tugs, strange periods of restlessness. You'll wonder about them! And there will be moments when something will suddenly stir and pass over your soul, like a breeze over water, causing just the very slightest ripple. Then it will be gone, leaving a curious residue of sadness and joy in you. Those will be hints. But you won't remember anything specific about here and us.*[1]

It's so true. We don't remember our spiritual beginnings until we hit a wall, and we begin to question the meaning of our lives. Then, as the following story illustrates, we start the journey of remembrance. This journey, often undertaken in confusion and desperation, becomes something ancient and holy—a pilgrimage. Somewhere along the road, we become aware of all those who have walked before us, clearing the path. We see our own part in that process of clearing the path for others as well. Eventually, we understand the paradoxical nature of the journey itself--that while we are struggling to reach our Source, our Source is, in fact, the Pilgrimage itself. It is as if Source, while holding us in love, illumines the way through our souls, from the inside out. We realize that we are both the journey and the traveler. This is the unfolding story of this book.

Straight out of college, George went to work with a large computer company based in Seattle. By the time he was 29 he was head of his own department and was making over $100,000 per year. At 33 he was promoted to director of Western sales and transferred to Dallas. For 3 years he absolutely loved his life. Everything he'd ever dreamed had come true. In fact he had far exceeded his wildest dreams, but then...

> *"I was really on the fast track—I was acquiring*
> *more prestige and influence daily. Yet, I didn't seem to*
> *be happy anymore. I loved the thrill of accomplishment,*
> *but I felt caught in it somehow. When I slowed down,*
> *I just felt the pressure to do more, to keep acquiring*
> *more knowledge and power, yet those things didn't mean*
> *anything to me anymore. I felt deeply disillusioned,*
> *and filled with a frightening yearning I couldn't name."*
> *(George)*

What do we do when we attain the Dream and it becomes meaningless and leaves us restless with yearning and looking for more? What do we do when we are unable to achieve the American Dream? Why do we cling to the dream to give us a sense of self-worth even when it no longer sustains us? How do we release the Dream when it is so frightening to let go? Who are we if we are not the Dream?

Pilgrimage of the Soul will take you on the journey of moving beyond the Dream into your deep authenticity and home to your forgotten Source. Each section of this book will cross new thresholds of expanding awareness and self-realization.

George's story illustrates the FIRST THRESHOLD of spiritual transformation—*I am an Awakening Self.* We cross this threshold when we become aware of a deep dissatisfaction and yearning. George brings down to earth all of the challenges and temptations of living in a world that is driven by ego power and how important it is to fully understand what that means at a deeply personal level.

In this first section, you will find chapters devoted to the topics of yearning, illusions of power, untying the knots that bind us, opening the heart, befriending darkness, and sensing energy.

As we come to the SECOND THRESHOLD—*I am a Spiritual Human Being,* we see that George has become much more aware of who he is. He could see the ways that he still struggled with his need for control in his life, and, at the same time, knew that his spiritual path was leading him beyond that kind of control.

He was startlingly aware of how much he was not really present to either himself or his life. In many ways, he just went mindlessly through the motions of daily activities. Going unconscious was like a slippery slope to him. It had helped him survive his childhood, and he had become very good at it. He often didn't know he wasn't present until he was centered again and then could feel the difference. But, later, his clarity would slip away; he knew something wasn't quite right, but couldn't name it.

> *"It's as though, when I'm not present, I forget*
> *what presence is, or how to get there. Then, I read an*
> *inspiring poem, or meditate, and I'm present again, and*
> *I realize that I've been absent—running on automatic*
> *pilot. My goal, now, is to keep coming back to being*
> *present."(George)*

This commitment to keep trying to be present is the hallmark of crossing the second threshold. You will find, in this section, explorations of the fears and joys of being present, becoming authentic, making intentional choices, and transforming the ego.

As we come to the THIRD THRESHOLD—*Beyond "I"*, we find George preparing himself to make this transition.

> *"Once again, I feel on the precipice, afraid of jumping in, and afraid not to. But, this time, I know that the only real choice is to leap. Not to do so would betray all of the inner work I have done so far. To plunge into this path now means really trusting that this process will take me where I'm supposed to go. I don't know if I'm ready for that kind of trust. It means that I'll have to open myself more, and I don't know if I can be my own genuine self all of the time. I'm so used to choosing which parts of myself I'll reveal to which person. It's become such a habit. Yet, I know how much I feel connected to the richness of my soul and to God when I meditate, and I really do want more of that connection all of the time. I know there is really no choice but to go deeper into my spirituality." (George)*

The hallmark of the third threshold is the commitment to trusting the deep spiritual process at work within us as we move beyond who we have known ourselves to be. You will find chapters exploring the ways of releasing self and trusting Source, the unifying, yet paradoxical, experiences of Oneness, and creativity, service and leadership.

How do the perceptions and experiences inherent in crossing each threshold affect how we think and feel about our lives? What does the living of this knowledge teach us about our selves and our relationship to the universe? Seeking answers to these questions is the essence of this book. It is designed for those who are awakening to their spirituality and to those who are well along in their journeys. Each chapter contains stories of our own personal experiences, and the men and women with whom we have worked. The meditations and self-reflection exercises following each chapter are those that we, the authors, have found helpful for ourselves and for our clients.

Crossing the First Threshold

I am an Awakening Self

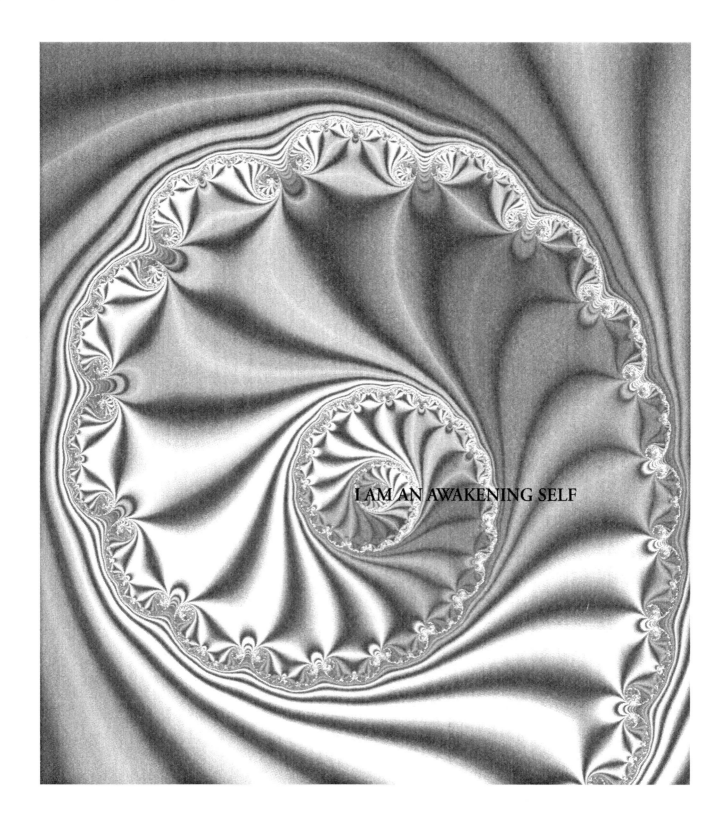

1

WAKING UP

*"The full open rose needs a stem
to grow on and out of."*
Andrew Harvey[1]

*"When I was in my mid forties I
was up to my ears in what I thought was
a "successful" life. I had two delightful
teen-age daughters, a long-term marriage,
and a thriving campus ministry with
young adults who were eager to explore
the depths of spiritual formation with me.
I was also meeting with individuals as a
spiritual director and listening intently to
their unique spiritual journeys, questions,
and longings.*

*In the midst of this busy and
intense life, my father died after a long
struggle with cancer. Soon after his
death, I began to experience an inner,*

subtle pull toward more solitude and silence. I found myself yearning for time alone to "let my soul catch up" and felt myself losing energy and becoming more fatigued with each passing day. My marriage became shaky while both of my daughters began to rebel in very different, and for one, dangerous ways. My prayer life, which had always been full of rich images and experiences, became dark and foreign to me. God seemed suddenly absent. As I entered more completely into this "dark night" time, I sensed that I would have to go deep inside myself to find meaning and authenticity in a life I no longer recognized as mine."
(Suzanne)

*   *   *

"My dissatisfaction with the fast-paced life felt as though it came out of the blue. I was working as a faculty member and chairperson of a department at a university. I went to work one day loving the work that I was doing and enjoying this position that I had worked hard to achieve. Then, the next morning, when I went into the office, I wondered what in the world I was doing there. Literally overnight, my whole perspective had changed. What had held meaning for me, what seemed to define me, now seemed to be irrelevant and empty. I felt that I was in a kind of shock. I couldn't figure out what was wrong with me that I could change so quickly. I had trouble focusing on my work. Once I got focused, I could still do what I needed to do and enjoyed much of it, but the meaning had gone out of it.

A few weeks later as I came out of the shock, I realized that my dissatisfaction had actually been growing since the death of my aunt, with whom I was especially close, several months before. During the infrequent times when I had slowed down, I had been overwhelmed with sadness and grief. At the same time, I was beginning to feel trapped in my work. I enjoyed the feelings of accomplishment, yet I felt pushed to achieve more. I felt as if I were running to keep up and to get ahead. I realized that I didn't know who I was if I wasn't running. I was afraid to look inside. What if there wasn't anyone in there? What would I do if I weren't engaged in this work? How would I earn a living?

At first, my way of coping with the sadness and fear was to ignore them and to bury them in more work. I bought a new house and arranged for new travels which, in retrospect, served as good distractions, but which made little difference in the long run. All my hard work and years of achievement had left me feeling fragmented, empty, and restless, and now I was without meaning. I had hit the wall and finally knew that I had to look inside myself for the real answers." (Sally)

Life's greatest challenges often force us to look more closely at the spiritual aspects of our lives. In our quest for purpose and meaning, we may be drawn to making life changes that bring us into greater alignment and harmony with our spiritual source, that is, with a force greater than ourselves. As this journey begins, we may feel a familiar tug, something we recognize we've felt our whole lives, though it may have been obscured by the demands of our daily lives. Often we feel this tug in a growing dissatisfaction in our work and relationships, where we have invested so much hope and may have already reaped many personal satisfactions and rewards. Surely work and relationships are important, but we find ourselves searching for something more, something to fulfill a deep inner longing that neither work nor our everyday relationships seem to satisfy.

We may first notice our growing dissatisfaction through feelings that if we are to be successful we must do more, make more, and do it all faster than anyone else. We measure our goals in quicker and better results. And we often find that this fast-moving, intense life fuels a sense of fragmentation and alienation within us because it leaves little time for reflection and self-awareness. We may feel a dissatisfaction that is *bone deep*, that goes beyond just feeling busy and overworked.

If you are experiencing any of what we describe here, rest assured that you are not alone. Many of us share this discomfort with the fast pace of life. When we do have time for ourselves, we want to be happy and have fun. We don't want to be "bogged down" with difficult emotions that so often surface when we slow down. Slowing down gives us the space to feel loneliness, fear, grief, inadequacy, and yearning. When we try to ignore these feelings, we contribute further to our growing dissatisfaction with our lives.

When we first become aware of our dissatisfaction, we look for something to satisfy it. We are often afraid to look inside because we don't know who we are in there, fearing that we will find nothing or, we won't like whom we find. So, we try to find something outside ourselves to make us feel better, such as a food, drink, spending money, travel, new lover, a new car, or some other new experience. We find, though, that nothing satisfies us for very long. We are forced to sit with the dissatisfaction until we are willing to look inside ourselves to find its source. Thus, starts the spiritual journey.

While the experiences that started our, Suzanne's and Sally's, spiritual journeys are different, they have common themes. We both experienced the loss of someone important to us. Our work, that had been life giving, suddenly felt dry and meaningless. All the ways we had employed for giving meaning in our lives, such as, prayer, travel and family life, no longer worked. "Success" no longer held any promises for us. We were left with deeply disconcerting questions: What do we do when we capture the American Dream and it leaves us empty and restless, believing that the "failure" we feel is the result of our own shortcomings rather than the dream's limitations?

The American Dream tells us that by our own efforts we can do and be anything we want. Our immigrant grandfathers and grandmothers came here because of the vision of a land of opportunity with its streets lined with gold. Through perseverance and hard work many of them made the dream a reality. The Dream continues to promise us personal success, financial security and happiness.

When we don't achieve the promises of the Dream we become disillusioned and disheartened. Rather than recognizing the Dream as an illusion, and therefore limited, we instead, feel that there is something lacking or at fault in ourselves. One limitation of the Dream is the illusion of personal entitlement…the idea that if we just work hard enough we are guaranteed happiness and our lives will have meaning. Another limitation is that because the Dream has become institutionalized in our culture, we believe that everyone can and should achieve it. This belief does not consider how our own personal path may lead in another direction. There is nothing wrong with achievement and success. Yet, when we depend on them to give us a sense of our own self-worth, we can find ourselves disillusioned because it may not nourish us deeply enough.

Tangled up with the American Dream is our Western religious tradition, primarily Christian, that teaches us that the "good life", as well as salvation, comes through self-sacrifice, faith, piety and striving for perfection. If we don't achieve the "good life" we are judged, or judge ourselves, to be lacking in faith or moral fiber. This sets us up to believe that the yearnings of our hearts are somehow selfish and unworthy. Thus, many of us learn to distrust our own experiences of our depth, and God or Spirit, and rely instead on the rules of religion to define our worthiness. Reliance only on dogma can become another dream full of illusion and limitation.

Our disillusionment comes about because the patterns of our human ego can no longer sustain us with the deeper nurturance we may require. The ego is our separate and personal sense of self. It is essential to our growing up as capable and knowledgeable adults. In order to understand the role of ego in our lives, let us take a short journey into the development of the level of consciousness that is our ego. The ego is but one of many levels of consciousness. Each level has its own identity, its own modes of knowing and being and awareness.

Patterns of Ego Consciousness

Out of the world of our spiritual Source, we humans emerge into the world of form, acquiring a human body. At first, we are not so separate from Spirit; then, as we grow and develop through childhood, adolescence, and young adulthood, we experience an increasing sense of individuation or separate identity. This separate, personal identity, is our human ego.

In order for humans to function well, the universe must be reduced to human size. We do this by continuously setting boundaries by our selective attention. We pay attention to certain aspects of our environment, thereby allowing those things into our consciousness. The things that we pay no attention to will not become conscious to us. These boundaries we set become patterns, or templates that give substance to our personal identities—our egos.

The **first of these patterns** laid down in childhood is the distinction between self and other. This is our most fundamental boundary.[2] This pattern allows us to develop a sense of ourselves as individuals and separate from those around us. It is the first unfolding of ego consciousness; it creates space for us—space between ourselves and everyone and everything else.

"I remember when my daughter was about two years old. She began to use the words, 'my' and 'mine.' It was fascinating to watch her begin to claim her separate self." (Suzanne)

With space comes the **second pattern**, a sense of time with its distinctions between past, present, and future. When we are very young, we experience only a present. Then, we gradually learn to look forward to a future event and to remember past experiences. In

Western culture, we learn to see our past--accomplishments, hurts, failures--as who we are, and project that image into the future. The present becomes only a stepping-stone to what we imagine our future to be.

"I'll never meet the right man for me, all I have
ever attracted are men who are already committed or
else are afraid of commitment. I have no reason to hope
that it will ever be any different." (Jane)

Knowledge of past, present, and future brings us into the **third pattern**, the distinction between life and death—between existence and nothing. This awareness generates a fear of death with its accompanying anxiety and the perceived need for control over life.

"I used to run and exercise several times a week
to keep my body young and to avoid disease. The
outcome was that I developed arthritis, and have to
slow down my physical activity and come to terms with
the limitations of my body." (Fred)

Because we cannot face the mortality of our bodies, we develop an inner boundary between body and mind, and we become primarily identified with our minds. Our attention becomes more focused on our intellect, and we lose awareness of our bodies and the development of its senses. This loss of the unity of mind and body, is immense, for within it, we lose our ability to be present in thought and feeling simultaneously, as well as our sense of being whole.[3]

The loss of our sense of unity has two major implications. The first has to do with our focus on our intellects. We tend to discount any aspect of ourselves that is not immediately obvious, or which does not fit what we consider to be our rational ways of thinking. These discounted aspects are, most often, our emotional nature, and our connection to a spiritual source.

"I enjoy problem solving, and I'm a good trouble shooter. I don't like it when other people get all emotional about a problem. It just makes things messy." (Dick)

"I think it's a bunch of woo-woo when people talk about making decisions based on intuition or divine guidance." (Kay)

The second implication has to do with our bodies. The body, as all material forms, is to be dominated and controlled by the mind. Again, by focusing our attention on our mental abilities, and not on our bodies and its sensations, we lose varying degrees of body awareness. With this loss, we are more likely to treat our bodies badly and unhealthily.

"I used to run my body until I was so exhausted I couldn't move. I would be so angry at my body for it's limitations. It wasn't until I tore a muscle, and had to go through rehabilitation that I realized how much I was abusing my body. Now I am more aware of my body's signals of fatigue." (Bruce)

With all of these boundaries comes a mind separated from its body—the ego's image of its self. Through young adulthood, we polish this self-image as we achieve the values of our culture. This image becomes our first sustaining identity as a human self.

Because our culture values and fosters the development of images, we create another pattern of separation in ourselves—between what is an acceptable self-image and what is not. Once again, this separation is created by our selective attention to what is most valued. All of the parts of us that don't fit the image we aspire to are usually ignored, or disowned. These disregarded parts of ourselves become the shadow within us—the aspects of ourselves we come to dislike and, perhaps, even fear.

"I am so unhappy. I work so hard to be the person others will like, but I don't seem to have very many friends. I have a few and I do have fun with them, but I wish I was more popular. I wish I could be like

other people--happy all the time. I hate myself when I feel
anxious and afraid that I won't be happy." (Charlotte)

Our developing egos do, by their very nature, bring us into limited, contracted, and fragmented lives. Yet, for all it's boundary setting, and despite its alienation from Spirit, the ego is the first level of our human consciousness strong enough to integrate its own development. This ego strength is the foundation upon which we commence our pilgrimage back to our home in the realms of Spirit.

Our journey of return begins when we feel discomfort and dissatisfaction with the world we have created for ourselves. Our urge is toward an expansion of awareness into greater consciousness. Up until this time, our ego patterns have limited our range of consciousness for the most part. Now our discomfort and dissatisfaction beckon us to expand into greater self-awareness. As we embark on this journey of expansion, we begin to realize that there is more to us than the self that we have experienced so far.

When we first suspect that our belief systems, the ways we see the world, are illusions that we ourselves have created or been taught, we experience feelings of disorientation, even dis-ease, darkness and disillusionment. The inner boundaries begin to crumble, and we start to see those shadow parts of ourselves that we have held at bay. We see that our identification with our self-image will no longer sustain meaning in our lives. We feel the pain that comes when all that we have believed about our lives starts unraveling.

These feelings, along with a changing perspective, were the indicators that took us, Sally and Suzanne, into ourselves and launched us into the deepening of our spiritual understanding. Along the way, we experienced shifts in identity that seemed to be thresholds into the greater dimensions of Spirit, and self-realization, that were unfolding in us. These shifts moved from very personal to beyond any personal sense whatsoever. Our affinity with our self-images gave way to the increasing urges of our souls, and we became reacquainted with the aspects of ourselves that we had disregarded or disowned. As we reclaimed our full emotional nature and our connection to Spirit, we moved into a deeper identity as a spiritual self. Then, after a while, even that identity dissolved into a sense of no personal self, a state lived in the fullness of soul and Spirit.

There were three thresholds to cross, places where we entered into areas of deeper understanding and meaning. This was new ground within our selves, with new sounds, new perspectives, and new rhythms. Throughout all of these changes, our spiritual practices kept the path clear to us. Using a spiritual practice was like wearing a path through the woods, so that it becomes easier and easier to follow, to get to that place of peace.

Here is a brief introduction to the three thresholds that we crossed. Each one opening to self-realizations that embraced all that had come before, and integrated it into a larger perspective.

The **first threshold** we cross is our acknowledgement of dissatisfaction with our lives. We begin asking deeper questions than our egos can answer. We may wonder, "Who am I?" "Why am I here?" What is my purpose in life?" "Do I have a soul?" "What is God? Is there a God?"

This questioning puts us in a profound quandary, as we realize that there might be more to ourselves than the image that we have carefully constructed and nurtured. Glimpsing, if only momentarily, the smallness of our egos, is terrifying. Yet, in spite of the fear, we are impelled to follow the trail of that which is greater. As we enter this sphere of experience, all past accomplishments, beliefs, and ways of being may seem meaningless and thus become fertile ground for examination. Here, too, we confront survival patterns based in fear, guilt, unworthiness, judgment and despair that dampen or block the deeper awareness trying to surface in our consciousness. As we do this inner work, our egos begin to undergo a transformation.

We cross the **second threshold** when we make a commitment to becoming consciously present and authentic. Here we release old patterns of separation within ourselves and develop trust in our inner process. Slowly, we become our authentic selves as we deepen our connection to spirit and begin to realize that we will become our

The First Threshold is our acknowledgement of dissatisfaction with out lives

The Second Threshold is our commitment to becoming consciously present and authentic.

soul's instrument of expression. Our changing egos are no longer in charge because we no longer have the need to control or direct our lives in the ways we have previously. We make a commitment to trust soul and Source to guide us.

We cross the **third threshold** when we realize that we have entered a state of being in which we have no more doubts, no more questions, no fears, no need to know. This can seem like a huge leap for us to make. Yet, there are small clues all along the journey that point to the possibility that this state of being exists in all of us. Some of us may glimpse this state in prayer or meditations in which we feel an expansion beyond ourselves. Others may have visual, auditory or other sensed extraordinary moments that make us feel deeply connected to all of life. Still others may experience this kind of connection through relationships, either individually or in community. We do not live in this state of being all of the time, but when we cross this third threshold, this state becomes our new foundation. We recognize it as the ground of our being, the place out of which our souls flow. Our ability to be present in this state of being becomes easier and more frequent over time. We become identified with it; that is, much of the time we no longer identify with "I", but rather our identity shifts to an awareness of being soul and Source. In this state of being, we feel the urge to express our sense of oneness out into the world, in our work, in our relationships and in service to others.

This book, then, is about the constantly changing, developing, and deepening human and spiritual beings that we are. It is about coming to a sense of hope and peace with all of the restlessness and longing within us and realizing that, when we can allow it, all of these movements bring us home to their source—our souls—our wholeness.

The Third Threshold is the realization of no more doubts or fears.

SELF REFLECTION

LIFE REVIEW

One way to personalize the material that you have just read is to do a life review. Looking back at each decade of your life, and using the matrix on the following page as a model, make note of the following:

- who are/were the memorable people in your life in each decade?
- what were the significant events in each decade?
- What was your experience of God, spirituality, the Sacred in each decade?
- What kinds of environments were conducive to opening your awareness of spirituality?
- Make or find a symbol that represents each decade for you.

Decades	0-10	11-20	21-30	31-40	41-50	51-60+
People						
Events						
Spirit-uality						
Environ-ments						
Symbols						

Notes

Notes

2

ILLUSIONS OF POWER

"When one is soaring on the wings of power,
one feels he has transcended suffering."
Mariana Caplan[1]

Janice thought she had it all—marriage, motherhood, and career. Her husband was a corporate vice-president and they had two children who were good students, both active in sports and music. Janice, herself, was a high school math teacher. She successfully managed her family life and career until her mother died.

"When my mother died, I felt like the rug was
pulled out from under me. I was going along, just loving
my life, and feeling really competent because I could
juggle it all. Then, all of sudden, I felt like I was falling
into a dark hole. Nothing seemed recognizable any
more, including myself. I found myself going through all
the motions of my busy life, yet unable to connect with
any of it in any meaningful way. This went on for a
couple of years, even after I felt that the grief had lifted.

*I realized I was yearning for something different in my
life. All the juggling now seemed to be exhausting, and
unfulfilling. I had always loved being needed, but now,
I felt drained and entrapped by all the demands.(Janice)*

Janice's story illustrates the first threshold of spiritual transformation — the awareness of a deep dissatisfaction and yearning. Her story brings down to earth all of the challenges and temptations of living in a world that is driven by ego power and how important it is to fully understand what that means at a deeply personal level. Our beliefs about how to succeed in life grow out of our cultural ideas and attitudes about self-image, power, and success. As Janice's story demonstrates, there are limits to ego power. Our carefully nurtured notions of success are often unmasked as illusions for us. Illusion is defined as something that deceives the senses or mind, for example by appearing to exist when it does not or appearing to be one thing when it is in fact another. Illusions are our false ideas, conceptions or beliefs concerning something. We may be taught or adopt certain ways of being that seem useful or important in life but that can become illusions and as such, they no longer serve us. In attempting to conform to the expectations of our families, culture or religion we can lose our selves in a dream that may not be our own. This is what was happening to Janice, and continues to happen for many of us.

For the past few centuries, humankind has been struggling with the ego's materially focused view of power. This perspective tells us that everything in the universe is derived from matter – that matter is the ground of all being. In this model, all of reality has been collapsed into physical reality. What cannot be seen, measured or logically thought out is something unexplainable that is to be avoided. We are conditioned to ignore our feelings, intuition and imagination. Humans are valued as machines that can reason logically and use language to communicate rational thought.

In spite of the materialistic beliefs about power, we are becoming increasingly aware of an emerging perspective. Advances in science have given us new information about the nature of the universe in which we perceive not facts and objects, but processes, movements, matter and energy. This new perception tells us that it is energy, not matter, that is the ground of all being and from which everything arises. To many scientists this energy is consciousness. What we now know is that matter is the material manifestation of forms of energy and consciousness, and not the other way around.

This new perspective validates and reconnects us with our feelings, imagination, intuition, and sensitivity; those parts of us that are not physical. It moves our consciousness beyond a materialistic philosophy. It brings us the realization that our materialistic way of thinking is not complete; however, it does manage to dominate how we function in the world. The idea that everything comes from matter is an illusion in the face of evidence that matter is instead only a form of energy.

Here are a few of the illusions that play out in our lives:

Illusion #1 – If it's not matter, it doesn't matter

If everything is viewed within the context of physical reality, then only matter exists. This means that earth and the human are valued only as matter. They are to be controlled, dominated, subjugated, and used as resources for power. If we are to be seen, then it becomes important that we look good. Keeping up appearances, a polished self-image, is a high priority. Material progress, productivity and looking good become the focus of human endeavor.

"Seeing is believing."

"Nevada is a great place to dump toxic waste. There's nothing there."

"You can't go out of the house dressed like that. What will the neighbors think?"

Illusion #2 – We are what we have

Because material wealth and possessions signal our competence and influence in the world, we want to acquire those things that

The Spirit shall look out through Matter's gaze
And Matter shall reveal the Spirit's face. . .
And all the earth become a single life.

*Sri Aurobindo in Savitri*₂

symbolize power and success. These symbols include wealth, position, titles, college degrees, the type of cars we own, where we live, the birth of a child, the success of one's spouse or children, or luxury vacations. Success in our culture is measured in how many and how much of the symbols of power we acquire. These symbols make our success visible. Visibility helps us to develop strong egos, and an opportunity to see how we can control and influence the world around us.

"Chicks are going to want me 'cause I have a hot car."

"With this new raise, I'll be able to buy a yacht."

"We're going to join a ski club this year, the one that all the Microsoft execs belong to."

"My husband just became corporate Vice President. Now we have to buy a new house to entertain his colleagues."

"I'm working all the overtime I can get. I want to be seen as a go-getter. I want to be president of this company."

All too easily, these illusions of power become a measure of our self worth. We imbue our symbols with so much meaning that we cannot imagine who we would be without them.

Illusion #3 – Knowledge is power

We have an insatiable need to know everything. Doesn't knowing things make us feel powerful? Don't we feel more in control or successful when we know why things are the way they are or why things happen the way they do? Striving for knowledge has become the work of our ego-driven intellect and we are drowning in facts about everything.

Because knowledge is so valued for the power it can wield, we pursue it with a passion, accumulating it like we do our material possessions. We forget that knowledge is more than facts - more than what our intellect tells us. Knowledge is also intuitive insights, wisdom, creativity, and imagination.

The illusion is that only intellectual knowledge is valuable and will make us powerful and successful. We measure our worth by how much we know. One of the ramifications of living this illusion is that our personal realities are fragmented. By valuing our intellect over other aspects of our selves, we learn to deny and distrust our other ways of knowing.

"One way I have power at work is by having more information than anyone else." (Ted)

"I've always relied on my intellect and my ability to logically problem solve to feel good about myself." (Betty)

"My son is addicted to the internet. Technology has given him lots of information, but I worry about his ability to get along with people." (Ray)

"Remember what you said to Tom this morning about the pricing? What did you think you were doing? What gave you the right to say that? I didn't want him to know yet. You're off this project as of now!" (Bert)

Illusion #4 – The world is black and white

The emphasis on logical thinking doesn't allow for the hues of gray that come with intuition and the colors of creativity. We are all exposed to variations of the following:

If things aren't good then they are bad or evil

If I am not right then I must be wrong.

Every problem has one right answer

If I am not a winner then I am a loser

Black and white thinking requires rigid conformity to a particular point of view that generates a judgmental attitude and in turn can cause aggression. We have all seen instances of road rage following the judgment of another driver's maneuver. Aggression on a domestic, national or world scale stems from this kind of thinking. This illusion pervades our institutions where, in order to be valued, seen as good and to become competent, we learn to conform to the rules of the institution. We can either conform and be rewarded or we may be judged as lazy, disruptive, or deviant. Black and white thinking doesn't take into account individual perspectives within any given situation.

> *"Your plan is too ambiguous. It leaves too much room for people to come up with their own ideas."* (John)

> *"If you elect me, I will never sign a bill that will raise your taxes." (Bill)*

> *"I don't pay you to come up with alternatives. I pay you to get the job done, and done right." (Robert)*

Illusion #5 – We are in control

The empowerment of the human self and its ego is of utmost importance. Ego-centered power, that is, power to control our environment as we see fit, is supposed to enable us to control how change occurs so that we can "handle it well". "Well" means that we always appear and act as if we are in control. If we can't actually control change, then at the very least, we are expected to appear as if we are in control of ourselves. It always comes back to reinventing our selves in times of change and doing whatever it takes to regain control of our environment.

> *"I can't afford to let everyone do what they want to do. The whole place would be in chaos. People basically need to have structure and order. They are more secure that way." (Claudia)*

> *"You have too much energy and drive. I think you would benefit from more structured supervision." (Greg)*

> *"You know, I could really be much more supportive of you on your next project if you were more solidly behind me and my ideas." (Morgan)*

Illusion #6 – Strong emotion should not be expressed

Deep feelings and intuitions are considered private and not to be expressed in front of others. They are to be judged shameful, and are to be held down, and overcome. If we can't manage to hold them in, or if holding them in causes anxiety, panic or severe depression, then we are seen to be weak, sick, eccentric, wild, or crazy. In this illusion of power, expressing deep emotion is characterized as "breaking down." The exception to this is the expression of anger and rage that arises when the need to control is extreme and thwarted. Anger is often seen when deeper feelings of hurt, grief and betrayal are not acknowledged and taken care of. We use our anger to fuel our desires to keep score and get even. Unfortunately, this is still very prevalent in our culture today, and has much to do with how we learn to become powerful, and with what power comes to mean to us.

"I don't care what you feel, just do what I say, or else." (Joe)

"I embarrassed myself at work, because I found myself crying over something the boss had said." (Harriet)

Illusion #7 – Wonder and imagination only belong in the realm of childhood

As children we always seemed to have a sense of wonder and awe—an awareness of the unseen as well as the seen. Imagination was just an ordinary part of our perception. This is who we were before being conditioned by illusions of power.

Our imagination and sense of wonder may have been nourished by a variety of experiences, such as nature, childhood fantasies, and the sensate aspects of religion—music, candles, Eucharist, and ritual. Perhaps you may have had nurturing people in your life that valued you as a child—just for who you were. Some of us found places where we were safe to be ourselves without limits, and could just *be* our feelings and sensations.

*"I would climb the tree in my backyard and sit
there for hours watching the leaves blow in the breeze
and the shadows change in the yard wondering, "Where
did all this come from? And Why?" (Suzanne)*

*"I used to lay on my back on the grass watching
the clouds and have the feeling that life was more than
I was living – that it was bigger, greater than whatever
was around me." (Sally)*

But, gradually, most of us are conditioned to hide our feelings, forget our memories and to numb our awareness. All of these patterns are ways we deny our wholeness. This is where our fragmentation starts.

*"When I first went to school, it was a shock to be
told that daydreaming was bad. I felt that I was bad."
(Sally)*

*"One of my elementary school teachers tore up
my art project because I made a green flower with a
pink stem. She said these weren't the right colors."
(Suzanne)*

Since the early sixties we have been conscious of the abusive nature of a model of power that views humans as machines. We began to question the standard of success that our culture held up to us that fostered the compartmentalization of our selves. We realized there was more to us than the parts valued by society. We began to hear messages from a variety of sources that validated this awareness.

The sixties called into question the elitism found in many of our institutions. Many of us know the experience of elitism that gives power and prestige to a small number of "successful" individuals whether within a fraternity of sorority, or within national organizations. If some of us are chosen to be in an elite group, we may bask in feeling special, set apart and more powerful. If we're not chosen, we feel that we have been put into the losers' camp. We not only lost to the competition, but we have lost some of our hard earned power.

The women's movement has made us aware of the imbalance of power in favor of the dominant white male culture. As women began to wrestle with this reality and strive for equal footing, they succumbed to the same illusions as men and their paths to success often looked just like those of their male counterpart's.

For some of us, our faith communities emphasized that grace is freely given and cannot be earned. However, even though we may have heard those words, it was difficult to internalize them when the more dominant cultural belief told us that we had to earn grace by being "good enough." "Good enough" meant being successful in the eyes of the world, or following a rigid moral code, or sacrificing our personal dreams for some form of service.

During these same years, advancements in Science supported our emerging awareness. Quantum Physics gave us new language, images, and ways of seeing that validated the wholeness of the universe and ourselves.

In spite of this knowledge and awareness, the illusions of power continue to be very seductive and compelling. It isn't that most of us don't know that they are illusions and haven't thought about how they affect our lives, but even when we see them for what they are, we continue to allow our illusions to direct our lives. They have become habits and patterns that we fulfill even when they no longer serve us. Eventually though, striving for power and its symbols no longer has meaning for us and we become disillusioned. We may even begin to recognize that, because of the illusions of power that we have held, we are being separated from our avenues of intuition and imagination that can bring us deeper insight and meaning.

"In spite of all I was achieving, I just wanted to
run away. I felt that I needed the time to see what
all this has been about. I wanted to know what had

driven me so far so fast. I wanted to understand why I felt so dissatisfied and why I had this underlying yearning for something else." (George)

SELF-REFLECTION

SEEKING THE TRUTH BEYOND ILLUSION

In order to discern the degree to which these illusions of power may have permeated our lives, we have to take time to reflect on our habits, patterns and beliefs about who we are. This process begins with creating a private place for reflection.

It is always surprising to learn how few of us have a private, sacred place in our homes, a place we can go to for a sense of tranquility and peace. At its best, such a space may encourage us to perform some small ritual, such as lighting a candle, or incense, or simply gazing at a picture, or listening to a particular piece of music, that is a reminder of the richness of our inner, spiritual worlds. It's a place where you might keep a journal, so that you can sit down and write your private thoughts and insights.

"In my home I have several nooks that are sacred spots for me. One is in my bedroom where I usually sit to write out my dreams or journal. On the wall is a small shelf with an icon or two, some small figures of women in prayer or meditation, a sitting Buddha, a candle and other pictures that touch my soul in some way and which change as I feel moved to change them.

I also have a small altar in my kitchen with the four elements of earth, air, fire, and water represented respectively by a small dish with earth in it, some bird feathers, a candle and a bowl of water. I have some rocks by the water and some other figures of nature (a carving of a river otter, some small turtles, acorns, seashells, etc.).

Both of these places remind me to take time to breathe, meditate, or center myself as the day progresses and offer a sacred place for quiet reflection"
(Suzanne)

"One of my sacred places in my home is a corner in a studio room. It's a room that is private from the rest of the house and very quiet. I can go there to be nourished by solitude and silence, to meditate and write in my journal, or to drum, or do creative projects. My corner has a comfortable chair; a table with a lamp, candles, and a pot with feathers; several stones; a couple of drums that I have made; and on the floor is a small rug that I brought home from India. The objects in my corner are here because they remind me of the ways my soul is touched, but they are not permanent residents. Sometimes, I exchange them for other objects which I gather from around the house, (a particular feather, picture, stones, an animal carving) that touch my heart in some way and that I want in my corner for a while."
(Sally)

The following ritual may help you to create a sacred space in your home that you can use over and over to gather yourself into the sacred space within you. You might want to bring a journal with you, in which you can make notes about your experiences.

- Find a quiet space in your home.
- Settle into a comfortable chair.
- Light a candle or some incense.
- Be intentional about giving yourself this time for reflection.
- Focus on your intention and let the busyness of your day just wait a little while.

When you feel you are settled in yourself, reflect on the following questions:

How are these illusions reflected in your life?

- If its not matter it doesn't matter
- We are what we have
- Knowledge is power
- The world is black and white
- We are in control

- Strong emotion should not be expressed
- Wonder and imagination only belong to the realm of childhood

What do you consider to be the signs of your success at this point in your life?

In what setting(s) do you feel most competent and self-confident?

In what parts of your life are you feeling dissatisfied?

Before you leave this sacred space, offer a word of gratitude, a gesture or a posture that honors this time of self-reflection, such as placing your hands together and bowing, making the sign of the cross, standing with your arms and hands open and let go of anything in you (i.e., fear, anxiety, self-judgment) that is no longer needed, or expanding your arms as you take in a deep breath while taking in peace and releasing burdens.

Pilgrimage of the Soul

Notes

3

YEARNING

> *". . . . . Spirit intercedes with sighs*
> *too deep for words"*
>
> Romans 8:26[1]

"I have a deep desire for affection. I want more affection from my husband, but I also want more affection from my friends and fellow workers. When I discuss this with my husband, he does become more affectionate. But then I find that that isn't really what I wanted. I think what I long for is a deeper kind of intimacy, a deep spiritual connection, with others and with God." (Mary Lou)

Yearning runs through us like an underground river. In reality, it is the voice of our soul trying to get our attention. It is yearning that causes us to stop and listen. It is yearning that shifts our orientation from an external focus to an internal one. We make this inward turn as we realize that our external success is no longer fulfilling, or the meaning of success has changed for us, or that we are looking for some deep peace in the midst of our busy lives. It is this dis-ease that causes us to pause and reflect upon the directions our lives have taken.

At first, we tend to interpret this yearning as some lack in our lives, or as depression. As a result, we try to externalize it rather than inwardly acknowledging it and giving it room to expand. So, we look around outside ourselves for something we think we need or want that will satisfy us and make us happy again. We may be satisfied for a while with a new lover, a new car, or a faster computer. Yet, the yearning persists and makes us restless.

"My relationship was good, but I became so restless and anxious. I thought, 'How can this be so good, when I feel so weird.' So, I decided to leave. But the restlessness and anxiety didn't go away. Several months later, I started another relationship, and, once again, the restlessness and anxiety drove me away. I feel such a yearning inside—I thought it was because I wanted a relationship. I can't figure out what is wrong with me." (Brandon)

Many of us think that if we can just be productive enough, the restlessness and yearning will subside.

"I was so excited about this project when I started. I threw myself into it, working day and night. Then, I took a few days off, and I don't know what happened, but I lost all my energy. Now I can hardly put one foot in from of the other. I'm getting nothing done. I feel this ache inside to keep doing more, but doing more doesn't make the ache go away. I don't know what is the matter with me that I get so depressed." (Amy)

When the yearning starts surfacing everywhere in our lives and becomes the focus of our thoughts, our conversations, our dreams, our vocational questions, and our relationships then it becomes the invitation to begin the spiritual journey in a serious way.

The first step we take is to allow ourselves to feel the yearning. We don't know anything--where the path is, where it is going, or why we are so compelled to find it. All we know is that we are restless and anxious until we start the journey. As we do, we see that there are many ways that yearning expresses itself.

> *"Yearning, for me, was a palpable experience of thirst for an immersion into the mystery of God. I tried to articulate what I was feeling to a close friend, and I began to read anything I could get my hands on about spiritual growth." (Suzanne)*

> *"It was like this all-consuming hunger and desire to be the source of myself. I didn't know how to think about spirit or God. I didn't know if it was inside me, outside me or where it was. . . but I felt that the path to it was to look inside myself for my source. (Sally)*

Sometimes, yearning shows up in dreams that may have overtones of death or loss.

> *"The dream that woke me one morning was of a gigantic black snake. The snake was to swallow my daughters and me. I was afraid, but willing to be swallowed because I knew that somehow I would live after the experience. I made myself as tall and narrow as possible so that I would fit in the snake's mouth. What made this dream profound for me was the understanding that the snake symbolized inner transformation, feminine energy and healing. I began to wait with hope and anticipation for change to occur." (Suzanne)*

> *"I dreamed that I was in a new, big building and all that was there were ladders and rafters. I was up in the rafters trying to keep my two dogs and me safe. For a long time, I was climbing ladders and walking beams trying to protect myself from the man outside who was trying to come in. . . the carpenter. When I awoke I*

Yearning runs through us like an underground river.

felt two things. First, that I was running from a person who could help me and, second, running from a person whose help I didn't want, but I felt too afraid and vulnerable to tell him so. I didn't want him building my house. I realized the house represented my changing internal structure that needed to be separate from the church in which I grew up." (Sally)

Yearning often shows up as longing for silence and solitude. Sometimes, we find ourselves in the silence of waiting—a fallow time, such as when the spring bulbs are in the ground, and there is no visible sign of growth. Sometimes, it is the pleasure of no words. Often there is simply no way to describe what we are experiencing, and silence is more comfortable.

Sometimes, the yearning manifests as a craving for a deep connection with nature. This craving can come as a desire to physically lie on the earth, to visually commune with trees or water. Taking time to camp or retreat in the wilderness can be healing because it provides a safe space to express one's feelings and emotions. The trees can witness what we feel without judgment. Staring at the wonder and timelessness of mountains and water can help us to gain a larger perspective on our lives.

Another way that yearning shows up is in a passion for making a difference in the world.

"I have this desire to do something great—to change the world in some way. I know I do this in my work with homeless kids, but I also long for a bigger arena that affects more people. This doesn't have anything to do with me being important, and, in fact, it scares me to think about it." (Marilyn)

These ways that we experience yearning are a normal part of the process in the development of our awareness of the soul, and all that we have forgotten about our soul's connection to the Source in our task of building a strong ego. The yearning is a beacon guiding us home; we just don't initially recognize it for what it is.

"As I began the two-year spiritual formation program, I met others who were on a similar journey. Their stories affirmed my own intense longing for love, acceptance, and a deep mystical relationship with the mystery I called God. I began to wrestle more and more with loving myself and with finding God within rather than outside my life and my experience." (Suzanne)

"The classes, counseling and group dynamics that I became involved in at the Psychosynthesis Center normalized my deep yearning, so that I wasn't feeling so crazy and different from everyone. Everyone in the Center was going through a similar process, and we could share our yearning and deep feelings with each other. I learned that my experiences were the usual experiences of those going through spiritual awakening. I no longer believed in the image of a God outside myself. But, I had yet to find the God within. What I did find was a renewal of hope and faith in the inherently sacred core of my being—my soul." (Sally)

Our challenge is to listen to the deeper voices that touch us in our yearning, and call us to heal the separation between self and soul. It is a courageous act to be willing to respond to our yearning and to give it room to expand.

SELF REFLECTION

ENGAGING IN A SPIRITUAL PRACTICE

An exchange between a master and a disciple:

> *"Is there anything I can do to make myself Enlightened?"*
>
> *"As little as you can do to make the sun rise in the morning."*
>
> *"Then of what use are the spiritual exercises you prescribe?"*
>
> *"To make sure your are not asleep when the sun begins to rise."*

Anthony DeMello₂

Learning anything takes practice. How do we expect to move along this spiritual journey unless we undertake the practice of our chosen path? Because spiritual practice takes us beyond our ego into deeper realms of consciousness, it helps us to loosen the knots of our habits, illusions and patterns of control.

Spiritual practice is about attentiveness, allowing our selves to be open and aware of the immediate moment. When we decide to undertake a spiritual practice, we must leave our expectations of what will happen and our judgments of "how well we are doing" behind. We give ourselves to a spiritual practice simply because, over time, it supports, informs, and helps us deepen the spiritual journey upon which we have embarked. We give ourselves to a spiritual practice trusting that our faithful intention to be present to Spirit will make us aware of the paths to follow and the invitations to deepen that Spirit extends to us each day.

There are many forms of spiritual practice including: sitting in silence in prayer or meditation, inspirational readings, communing with nature, using mantras or chants, drumming, writing in a journal, engaging in expressive arts, and walking meditations. The kind of practice we choose is of less importance than the fact that we frequently and regularly return ourselves to it.

Spiritual practice is not a panacea for emotional turbulence, nor will it smooth away our restlessness and discomforts. Our discomforts will continue for a long time. "Until we are deeply and more stably into the transpersonal realms, we will always want to try the next technique, the next teacher, the next approach."[3] Our egos tend to rebel against the solitariness of meditation or prayer. The ego is afraid that sitting in present-centered awareness will take us beyond ego's control, and this fear can show up as restlessness, boredom, and anxiety. Yet, our practice teaches us to become friends with our boredom, restlessness and fears.

The whole goal of a spiritual practice is to give us a method by which we can open to our Source and heal all of our separations.

CHOOSING A SPIRITUAL PRACTICE

Michelle loved walking in nature. It was where she felt her heart opened up in a way it didn't do in church or even in meditation groups. She discovered her daily practice consisted of a walk in the woods near her home. She learned walking meditation and during these walks she began to feel that her mind let go of everyday worries and concerns, and she was filled with feelings of freedom, gratitude and love.

Judi enjoys reading poetry. It touches her heart in a way that takes her out of her everyday busyness. Each morning she reads poetry and then responds to it be writing in her journal. This morning ritual has become her spiritual practice.

Mark went to a workshop on Centering Prayer. He found in this silent form of prayer a place of comfort for his restlessness. In this silent form of prayer, he sat and opened himself to God's presence without expectation. Sitting this way for fifteen minutes every morning became his spiritual practice. He found that the silence centered him and prepared him for the day ahead.

Music was the spiritual language for Diane. In the evening she plays a favorite CD, and just sits and listens. The music takes her into peacefulness, gratitude, and joy.

• If you don't yet have a practice, consider the following

How can the soul fulfill its purpose if we are not listening?

questions: What is it in your life that speaks to your heart and connects you with something greater than yourself? Is this something you could do or sit with or visit on a regular basis?

- Choose a practice that touches your heart and make a commitment to do it daily or two or three times a week, every week. Be faithful to the rhythm of your practice. If it seems to grow stale after a while, don't give up; rather, try to settle into it more deeply and trust that the practice is doing its work.

- What sensations and feelings are you aware of as you connect with your spiritual Source? Make notes in your journal, if you wish, to help you be attentive to your sensations and feelings.

Everything in life is meant to stretch me beyond my superficial self to my better self, to the Ultimate Good.

Chittister[4]

Our spiritual practice is about stretching us into our yearning and beyond.

God speaks to each of us as God makes us, then walks with us
silently out of the night.
These are the words we dimly hear:
You, sent out beyond your recall, go to the limits of your longing.
Embody me.
Flare up like flame and make big shadows I can move in.
Let everything happen to you: beauty and terror. Just keep going.
No feeling is final. Don't let yourself lose me.
Nearby is the country they call life. You will know it by its
seriousness.
Give me your hand.

        *Rainer Maria Rilke*₅

Notes

Notes

Pilgrimage of the Soul

Notes

4

LOOSENING THE KNOTS

"Desires come, my wishes and longing.
I am tied up, knot on top of knot."

Rumi₁

For a while I was part of a meditation
system. My teacher often referred to the "knots of our
conditioning" from which meditation would free
us. What I realized over time was that I was being
challenged to become free of my fears, which arose
whenever I felt myself stepping out of the bounds of my
previous beliefs, and expected behaviors. I felt as though
I couldn't even determine how I might want to think or
behave, because the fear loomed so large. As time went
on, I learned to just let the fear be, and not run from it.
The more I could allow the fear, and continue to find my
own ways of self-expression, the less fear I had." (Sally)

As we begin to uncover and give space for our yearning, we discover that this longing is inviting us to undertake the "journey of return" back to our spiritual Source where there are no separations.

However, we may have some difficulties in following where our longing may be inviting us, because we are "tied up in knots."

"When my daughter entered treatment for drug and alcohol addiction, I began to attend some ALANON meetings. I was terrified that I could do nothing to stop her from engaging in seriously life-threatening behavior. I was paralyzed with fear and at the same time "knotted up" in engaging in the same kind of useless rescuing behavior over and over again. I gradually came to face my fears, I learned that I could not cause, control or cure her addiction. One night I dreamed that a tangled mass of yarn with which I was wrestling had become disentangled…I awoke feeling a sense of peace and freedom." (Suzanne)

Our knots are the results of the patterns in which our egos develop into a strong personal sense of self, giving us definition, structure and self-image. Our knots are comprised of the beliefs, the emotional dynamics, and behavior that we develop in order to acquire power, knowledge and some measure of control in our lives. As we commence the spiritual journey, our yearning challenges these knots, and we begin to push against the constraints that our patterns have put upon us. As a result of giving our yearning room to expand so that we come to know it, and following the pull into silence and self-reflection, the knots that we have tied to develop the ego begin to loosen.

As these knots loosen, our beliefs and behaviors change, and the underlying fears that held them in place rise. Learning to face these fears is how we begin to unravel our knots.

There are three basic knots that are created by our ego patterns:

The knot of believing that life is certain and predictable

As this knot loosens, the fear of change and loss of control surfaces. How can we be in control if we don'tknow what lies ahead?

We begin to be aware of what the world has been telling us every day—that it is a very unpredictable place, in spite of our wanting and trying to hold on to a world of certainty. In order to deal with uncertainty we have to go deeper into ourselves than our egos-- we have to come down out of our heads. We begin to forge linkages, however tentative, with our hearts. When we do, our foundations are shaken because we are entering the realm of the unknown where we can no longer predict what will happen. We have no idea who lives beyond the ego until we dare to engage in self-reflection. Many of us fear that if we go inside, we won't find anyone home, or we won't like the person we find there. Even the idea of going into self-reflection can give us anxiety and fear? And for good reason, we are putting ourselves into a mysterious place, not knowing what the outcome will be. We fear losing our identity, our primary relationships, our vocations, our friends, and maybe our connection to reality as we have known it.

"Who will I be? Will anyone still know me, and love me? Will I lose my relationships? Will I lose my friends? I was afraid I would change so much that no one would recognize me, or like me anymore. Along with this, I was afraid that I would need to be doing other work. And, because I had no idea of what this might be, I was frightened." (Sally)

"In my self-reflection, I felt myself letting go of my need to be affirmed through my marriage, my friendships, or my work. Each time I allowed myself to sink into this 'letting go', I would feel a surge of fear. What if, in becoming more authentic, I had to let go of my marriage, my long time friends, and my work that

meant so much to me? It was hard to imagine surviving without those relationships." (Suzanne)

Self-reflection is not comfortable in the beginning. We have to be willing to persist in order to move through and beyond our fears and other emotions that come to the surface.

"When I first sat in solitude and silence, I was overcome with the anxiety of going into the unknown. As I persisted in sitting, though, I learned that I could move through the anxiety to a deeper place of comfort. This deeper place seemed to be the home of my yearning. After several weeks of daily sitting the anxiety dissolved, to be replaced by sadness, grief, or whatever other feelings I was harboring. I learned repeatedly that I could move below even these emotions to a deeper, peaceful place." (Sally)

"Whenever I got alone and quiet, tremendous grief would surface and I would find myself in tears. I had to allow the grief to have its way before I could experience other emotions and hear other voices from my heart and soul. Over time, as the grief abated, silence became a safe and healing place. (Suzanne)

"Images of my childhood abuse often surface during times of silent meditation. It is terrifying. I have had to learn to call on God's protective presence to accompany me into the mystery of silence so that I can move beyond old trauma and fear and allow the yearning of my spirit to speak to me of new ways of being."
(Alex)

The more we are able to hear the voices of our yearning that tug at our beliefs about predictability, the more we are able to move into the place of mystery, and trust that we can survive in the unknown. What we will ultimately discover is that we can be free of the burden of this drive for predictability, and when this happens we open more fully to our lives.

We cannot devise specific plans for a spiritual journey and just achieve them. There are no individual maps for this internal adventure. These deep journeys are not logical and rational; they are holistic multidimensional creative processes that are purely experiential and therefore open us up to possibility and uncertainty.

These experiences can often come in dreams, or in extrasensory perceptions. Sometime we can only know in hindsight, through our actual experiences, what our journeys are about for us, and the meanings they hold. These experiences pique our imaginations, and touch our hearts with a sense of the sacred.

"The grove of birch trees in my back yard are a cathedral for me. One day as I was gazing at the trees, they became a vision of white energy within which I could see in bold relief all of the birds twittering among the branches. As I continued to watch, the trees shifted again into many hues of green and the birds became golden. Then, they shifted back into my familiar, regular trees. As I sit with these trees, they bring me to sacred dimensions of myself." (Sally)

"I had a dream about giving birth to a child and then giving it up for adoption amidst the loud protests of family and friends. As I lived with the dream, I felt it was a way in which God was speaking to me. I began to look around in my conscious life for what I had given birth to that I might be willing to give up. After some time, I found that this dream, and subsequent dreams with the same theme, confirmed my sense that it was time to leave my current ministry (to which I was greatly attached) and take a sabbatical." (Suzanne)

As we begin to understand that we don't know with certainty how life will evolve, we listen to a deeper sense of integrity that tells us that the journey is no longer about skill development, strategic planning, and being in control. While we don't know what the entire journey is about yet, we begin to trust our own spiritual experiences and the hope and joy that comes from them. They can impart a sense of euphoria that can last for days or weeks.

The knot of feeling that we are not acceptable and lovable.

This belief leads us into trying to be who others want us to be for fear that we are not loveable as we are. It is about having the perfect self-image. Doesn't it seem as though we constantly have to change to meet someone else's expectations—our spouse's, our children's, our boss's, God's? As a result, we tend to believe that who we really are is not acceptable. Our fear of not being loveable holds that belief in place and keeps us in a pattern of adapting to the whims of others. In addition, this fear creates a critical, judgmental internal voice with its own set of expectations of what makes us acceptable to others.

> *"I should be able to work with people in recovery, since that is part of the covenant of my faith community. However, my father was an alcoholic and I feel re-traumatized when I have to be around people like him. I'm afraid my community will not accept me if I tell them how this work affects me and that I don't want to do it." (Linda)*

> *"When I make mistakes, I feel as though my stupidity is exposed for all to see. I ruminate over it for days, beating myself up for being so stupid." (Peter)*

> *"I have a desire to be led into a meditative practice. But when I do meditate, I feel guilty spending this time on myself. Spending time on my family is the top priority." (Joan)*

Loosening the knot of this belief opens you up to learning how to accept yourself just as you are. You begin to see the underside of yourself—this person who has worked so hard to find your place in this world. Perhaps you encounter characteristics that you don't like and that you judge as not good enough. Yet, even these characteristics display beneficial qualities, such as strength, determination, and perseverance. As you see these qualities that reside on the inside, you begin to appreciate the complexity of your human nature. As a result, you start to feel compassion for your struggles.

"Ever since I was a child, I was told that I was too much—too loud, too exuberant, too passionate. So I learned to dampen and subdue those expressive parts of myself. Then, in midlife, I felt stuck. I couldn't suppress myself any longer, but it felt way too risky to let my real self out. Finally, I had to. Otherwise, I felt as if I would explode. As I began to accept my passion and exuberance, I came to love it and found that it enriches my life." (Sally)

"When I was young, I enjoyed being physically strong. When I became an adolescent it was no longer acceptable to be physically strong and female. When my own daughters became adolescents, they were involved in sports, and took pride in their strengths. Watching them, I began to reclaim my body and worked to be physically strong again. I love being a physically strong woman." (Suzanne)

As we become more of our authentic selves, many of our superficial values drop away and we do change. And sometimes friends and loved ones may not understand why we are behaving differently. Loosening the knot of this fear means that we may be no longer willing to adapt to others if it requires a sacrifice of our integrity and authenticity. As we become aware of our authenticity, we know it as a possible source of internal power and self-esteem that does not depend on external recognition.

The knot of believing that we can protect ourselves from vulnerability by being closed.

This belief can take many forms, such as being the peacemaker to avoid conflict, keeping silent about things we are passionate about, or doubting and hiding our own perceptions. So when we first open ourselves to ourselves in self-reflection, we feel frightened of our vulnerability and we fear being visible, and thus vulnerable.

> *"I was meditating with a group. Every time I meditated. I cried my way through the meditation. I felt like I was crying for the world. I had no words for this experience, only tears. I was also deeply ashamed that I was doing this publicly." (Sally)*

Even as we sit in silence and listen, we may feel too vulnerable to trust what we hear. It can feel risky to act on what inner voices tell us. Some of us may have learned that expressing our true perceptions might bring us into conflict with others who are important to us in one way or another and perhaps threaten our sense of personal safety.

> *"I would get so furious with myself for not speaking my mind to my husband, for fear of ridicule. I wanted to have enough courage to speak my truth without fear of reprisal. Finally, I learned that my feelings were the feelings of powerlessness that many women have. That made me angry for all women, and from that anger came courage to be myself." (Suzanne)*

> *"Right after I moved out of my first apartment, the landlord called and told me that I owed him an additional $500 dollars because he said that I left the place a mess. I was shocked because I had painted the apartment and left it cleaner than I had found it. Even though I felt terrified, I called him back and told him that I would take him to court if he didn't rescind in writing his request for more money. I told him that I could document evidence of rats, cockroaches and filth in the apartment when I moved in. After some intense discussion, he backed down. I felt so empowered that I was able to speak my truth in the face of his intimidation." (Rachel)*

It takes time and continued practice to loosen this belief and allow the empowerment of being open to take the place of feelings of vulnerability.

Our forays into the unknown loosened our dependence on our minds as the only source of all valuable information.

As we work on changing these beliefs, we begin to dissolve our ego boundaries and separations. We search for deeper moorings that will anchor us.

Self-pity, self-doubt,
I acknowledge you.
I will not hate you.
You are part of me.
I will not push you away.
I will sit with you and keep
you company.
I will have my hand on
your heart.
I will not deny you.
I will not forget your grief.
You are my secret sister.
Are you afraid I will leave
you in the dark?
Come with me into the
room.
Whisper in my ear.
Put your tiny hand around
my neck, those fat rosy
fingers.
Your body along my ribs, fit
to me.
I can carry you monkey
fashion,
Your head a small cup on
my neck.

Toi Derricote[2]

SELF-REFLECTION

LOOSENING YOUR KNOTS

"Sometimes, I am afraid of all the changes going on within me, I often feel that my whole life is a kaleidoscope just waiting to be stilled so that a design comes into focus. But I am not still; rather I feel myself constantly shifting and this scares me. What helps me to feel better is to sit among the big trees in my yard, and to feel their stillness and constancy. They give me strength, and my fears subside. (Sally)

"I find that the fears of what change will bring surface when I find ways to be apart from the usual world I inhabit. That means I may be taking a walk, or staring out the window early in the morning before my day begins or sitting in my garden listening to the birds and smelling the breeze. In these solitary times and places I try to give space for my fears and to name them. By identifying them I get a better perspective. The fears become more manageable and not so overwhelming. Then, I often take note in my journal of what I have discovered about myself." (Suzanne)

As you enter your time of self-reflection, become aware of what your inner self might reveal as you consider your fear of change. Even though you may resist doing this, or have a sense of "fear and trembling" about it, be assured that you don't have to stay in the place of fear and discomfort to which your reflection may take you. You might want to give this type of reflection only an hour or two a week. Then afterward, engage in something that lightens your spirit. (Meet a friend, go to a movie, etc.)

Ask yourself the following questions:

1. What are the fears that surface when I contemplate a change in my life or in myself?

For example:

- "What will happen to my marriage if I undergo the inner changes of this spiritual journey?"
- "What if I change so much that I lose my friends?"
- " What if I change and need to leave my work with all its prestige and financial security?"

2. How do I respond to these fears?

For example:

- "I push them down and ignore them"
- "I get busy so I don't have to think about them"
- "I feel them, but I get overwhelmed, and then I try to distract myself with food, television, or I call up a friend."
- "I take them to my counselor or my spiritual director."
- "I write in my journal until the fear subsides."
- "I go for a long walk until I feel better."
- "I sometimes paint or sculpt my fears. When I paint them, I see how huge I can make them, often making them into murals, Then, I paint clowns into them."

Offer a word of gratitude, a gesture, or posture that honors this time of self-reflection.

Pilgrimage of the Soul

Notes

5

DISCOVERING THE DARK

"Give me a candle of the Spirit, as I
Go down into the deep of my own being.
Show me the hidden things. Take me down to the spring
Of my life, and tell me my nature and my name.
Give me freedom to grow so that I may become my true self-..."

George Appleton[1]

"I awoke one night in an agony of fear and grief. I
felt the need to pray, but I could not find any words to offer.
I didn't even know what to pray for. The darkness was com-
plete." (Suzanne)

The descent into darkness is an inherent part of the spiritual journey. Each of the world's spiritual traditions tells us of periods of profound and unsettling suffering that can precede, accompany, or follow the early stages of spiritual awakening. St. John of the Cross called it "the dark night of the soul,"[2] while other traditions refer to it as the desert, soul sickness, or the wilderness. This darkness is the suffering of the ego as it realizes for the first time that it is not the center of our being. *"It is the disturbing experience of recognizing, perhaps for the first time, how far we are from the truth.* "₃

The depth of this awareness is often accompanied by despair and disillusionment. There is literally nothing we can do in this darkness except to let go and surrender to it. In doing so, we pass a point of no return and our egos begin to erode and crumble.

One of our early experiences of the dark night can be a loss of the sense of connection with our Source. St. John of the Cross describes part of his suffering as stemming from the fact that he once caught a glimpse of God and then lost it.₄ We may experience a dark night time as a stripping away of customary ways of knowing our Source and finding meaning or purpose in life. It can be an experience of emptiness or void.

With our loss of spiritual connection we feel a great alienation, emptiness and a lack of all of the good feelings our spiritual practice had brought us. Gone are the feelings of joy and euphoria. Prior to this decent into darkness, we often felt that we, through all of our effort, were in control of our spiritual journey. All we had to do was to put ourselves in a posture of receiving what Spirit had to offer and it would come to us. Now, all of our efforts seem of no avail and we are powerless to change our situation. Because there is nothing we can do to feel closer to our Source, it can be a time of great anguish and despair. This plunge into our depths changes the focus of our spiritual practice from doing to allowing. We can only sit and wait for Spirit to lead us. We are waiting to see how that will happen.

"In the darkness came a voice, 'So, do you want to dance?' I was incredulous – what a question! The invitation came again, 'Do you want to dance?' Tears streamed down my face. 'Yes, yes, I want to dance, but I don't know how anymore!' 'I will teach you', came the response. My heart was flooded with a sense of comfort and hope...an incentive to continue to walk the dark

path, not knowing how or what would guide my feet through this fog of unknowing." (Suzanne)

> *"Whenever I would feel most lost and utterly powerless, my name was called in my sleep. 'Sally', 'Sally', it would call. It would startle me awake each time, seeming so real that I felt compelled to look around the house to see who had called. Yet, there was a quality of spirit to the experience, an interiority to it, that told me it came from deep in my soul, so that I felt seen and acknowledged even in my abyss. These name calling episodes gave me hope, and I would surrender to the darkness once again." (Sally)*

We literally sit in darkness with the debris of our patterns and our anxiety about being in this void. "What did I do wrong in my practice that brought me here?" "Maybe I didn't pray hard enough." "Maybe I didn't meditate well enough." "What do I do now to get back on my path?" Such thoughts are a common response to the shock of our new surroundings. Rest assured, you didn't do anything wrong. This darkness is Spirit at work within you.

This darkness signals a radical re-orientation where our Source, rather than our self, becomes the center of our life. It signals the beginning of letting go of self as a possession and of letting go of our dependence on proving self-worth. Rather, we begin to discover that we are a gift, born into the world so that the Source can be active through us. We also begin to learn to let go of others as possessions. This shift in orientation is a movement from logical problem-solving to deep contemplation where answers are illusive and may come in surprising ways.

Some of us are brought into darkness by external circumstances, such as the loss of a loved one, illness, loss of financial security, or loss of meaning in our lives. The darkness is such an inherent part of the spiritual journey that sometimes we only need to give ourselves time away from the our ordinary life in order for it to surface.

We have fallen into the mystery of our source.

A hallmark of the darkness is that we are unable to generate the spiritual experiences that once came to us so easily

"I went to a retreat where no one knew me. There were no constraints on how people saw me or on how I saw myself. I sat under a tree and started crying, 'What is this thing?' I remember thinking that I had to give 'it' permission to come forth. I screamed inside 'OK, OK'. I had done six years of 12-Step work (twice a week) and that was waning. I was getting scared because it was no longer enough. This gateway had appeared three other times in my life, but I was never ready to respond. Each time the openings came around there was more darkness before me, but I kept pushing it down. I had to come to a place where I could make decisions based on the value of myself. I had to value myself enough to move deeper into the darkness." (Mary)

Some of us end up in the abyss due to life's developmental transitions such as children leaving home, menopause, retirement, or loss of a dream, and start the spiritual journey from that place.

"Menopause and my work drove me to this place of deep despair. None of my ways of dealing with people worked anymore. I sought help and the counselor I found has helped to understand that I am in a place of great spiritual darkness. I realized that the pain I feel is the pain of my whole life. So, I am taking each thing and looking at it, and letting it go. I am aware of a spiritual depth in me that I haven't known before." (Moira)

"The business I had worked so hard, for so long, to build into a flourishing enterprise folded due to changing economic times. This was a terrible loss for me. I struggled with the questions, 'What will I do now?' 'How do I want to live the second half of my life?' 'What would continue to give my life meaning?' These questions caused me to go deeper to find answers that felt true to me. But I found myself in a dark place with

no answers. I had lost my dream, and had nothing to
replace it. As I began to realize that the failure of my
business did not mean that I was a failure as a person, I
began to be more at peace in this dark place." (Grant)

How do we learn to live in darkness when we expect and are expected to live in light? Opening to the darkness is counter to all of our conditioning. Our Western culture, our Christian theology and New Age spirituality, teach us that if we do it right, we will be rewarded by the culture, or by God, or by the Universe. Thus the time of darkness is often seen as a failure of faith and will. When perhaps instead, it is our yearning manifested in an aching desire to know and be known by the Source of our being. We have fallen into the mystery of our Source where we enter the process of being transformed and re-patterned.

"My spiritual director suggested I learn to
befriend the Darkness. That felt like a radical idea. It
meant that there must be something to connect with in
the dark…some unseen, un-sensed, unknown presence.
My path now became one of sitting companionably in
the mystery of this presence to see what it had to teach
me." (Suzanne)

"I began to ask, 'What if this darkness
isn't empty after all? What if it is full of energy more
subtle than I can sense yet? What if in my meditations,
I allow myself just to sit in the darkness, relax into it,
and open myself to it? What might I become aware of?'
This is what my meditations became." (Sally)

Though this darkness may last a long time, or feel unending while we are there, it is important to remember that the transformations that occur over time change us forever, and lay the ground work for the spiritual being we are becoming. The darkness is a call to us to new possibility, new meaning, and new direction. It not only gives us more interior freedom and greater compassion, but also prepares us to give birth to hope and newness in the world.

What to do in the
darkness
  Go slowly
  Consent to it
  But don't wallow in
it
  Know it as a place
of germination and
growth
  Remember the light
  Take an our-
stretched han d if you
find one
  Exercise unused
senses
  Find the path by
walking it
  Practice trust
  Watch for dawn

    Marilyn Chandler
      McEntyre[5]

SELF-REFLECTION

NAVIGATING THE DARKNESS

The importance of making time and space for this experience of darkness cannot be underestimated. In fact, we are almost compelled to make space for it since it can be so all consuming. We both had a spiritual practice that served as a container to hold us steady amid all the inner turmoil.

"The practice that sustained me during my "dark night" time was a daily time of centering prayer or meditation. I literally hungered for this time of prayer without words or images. As I began each daily period of silence, I gave consent for the Source of the Universe to come and be present with me. Though I didn't feel anything, I trusted that in the silence, the listening and the waiting something was taking place to prepare me to be aware of internal patterns that might be shifting, insights that might come through nature or other people, and other signs of hope or inklings of light. My spiritual director encouraged me to rest in this seemingly fallow time and to be faithful to my meditation. I found over several months, that this practice kept me centered and increased my trust in the unknown, sense-less movement of the darkness."(Suzanne)

"During my time of darkness, I was doing a meditation that focused on the light in my heart. I meditated for an hour each morning and thirty minutes each evening. This meditation, and my commitment to it, kept me grounded during this time of internal upheaval. In fact, most of the time early on, I clung to this practice as a sort of lifesaver. I sat, just focusing on the light in my heart that I couldn't see, opening myself to whatever awareness might come. I knew that I had to somehow trust this deep process at work within me, and

this practice of meditation kept me steady in that trust and open to Spirit. This particular practice continued for several years. I found that it opened my heart and changed me in many subtle ways. I felt more internal empowerment, which allowed me to be softer with myself and others. I knew that I was becoming more authentic."(Sally)

If you could find something that symbolizes your experiences of hope and trust as you wait in your darkness what would it be?

"I was going out of my front door one day to take a walk, trying to shake my darkness and despair. And there at my feet was a Cooper's Hawk feather. As I picked up the feather, the word 'hope' came to mind. I felt my heart open and I felt hopeful for the first time in weeks. Because these hawks feed on birds in flight, this feather became a symbol for me of just trusting that I would be nourished by the air of Spirit during this time of intense inner change." (Sally)

"During my time of darkness I created a ritual for letting go, trusting, and waiting. I had been reading Psalm 139:1-18, and the story of the woman at the well from the fourth chapter of the Gospel of John. (John 4:1-39). Both the Psalm and the woman's story reminded me of how intimately I was known and loved by God. I bought a small bowl, filled it with water and placed it on a beautiful cloth on my kitchen table. The water represented for me the womb of God—the place from which I have come and where I was infinitely known and loved. Beside the bowl, I placed a small dish of colorful stones that I had collected. When I needed to let go of my fear of the darkness, or my impatience with waiting in the dark, or my fear for another, I chose a stone, named the fear, and dropped the stone in the

She waits without answers, trusting God for the nourishment she can't produce herself. making covenants with the unseen new.

Sue Monk Kidd[6]

water. This ritual symbolized for me the releasing of my fear, and the way I wanted Spirit to nurture and hold me." (Suzanne)

Take your symbol into your spiritual practice as a sign of hope and trust that Spirit is with you in your darkness.

Notes

Pilgrimage of the Soul

Notes

6

OPENING THE HEART

> *"Openness is the door through which*
> *wisdom travels and contemplation begins."*
> Joan Chittister[1]

"*Every time my grandchild hugs me or climbs up into my lap, I am overcome with love and tears fill my eyes.* " *(Nancy)*

"*My dog has the most soul-filled eyes. When he looks at me with love, I feel my heart open, and I am touched.*" *(Sally)*

"*When I worked on a project for people who were homeless, their resilient spirits and stories touched my heart. For example, one woman had fled an abusive relationship taking her three children with her. Now, after months of job training and counseling, she had work and was ready to move out of the shelter and into*

*her own apartment. She was so grateful and so proud,
and I was deeply touched." (Sara)*

What is it in your life that touches your heart? A hug from a child, beautiful music, a deeply moving story, a look of connection from a loved one; all these are ways our hearts can be touched. When we feel touched it is our heart opening. As our hearts open, we often are aware of feelings of joy, compassion, comfort, connection or sadness. Tears or laughter can signal this opening.

For some of us, opening the heart feels too risky.

"I can't remember the last time my heart was touched."

"It's too scary to open my heart."

"I will feel too vulnerable if I open my heart."

*"My heart is full of grief and rage and I could be
consumed by it."*

How do we open our hearts? First of all, we can't *make* our hearts open. Rather we *allow* them to open when we are deeply touched and we feel the emotions that are elicited. The heart is the doorway to our authentic self. We make a commitment to wait for, to accept, and to listen to what our hearts tell us. We let go of having to control the internal knots we've made to protect our hearts. As these internal structures are loosened we feel our foundations shake and crumble and we have to be willing to live in the temporary disorientation that results.

*"I feel like I am standing on shifting sand. I miss
the sense of certainty I used to know." (Jody)*

In order to anchor ourselves internally in a place that is deeper and more enduring than our crumbling foundation, we rely on our spiritual practice. Your spiritual practice will be unique to you, comprised of the tools that you find most helpful to keep you centered as the inner journey deepens. For instance, to give substance to their self-reflection some people journal, write poetry, stories or music. Some people have a particular prayer or meditation that they use while others use drawing, painting, or sculpture. Some use body movement or dance and others feel most drawn to self-reflection when they are out in nature.

Some of us just sit with a question:
"What is my heart's desire at this time?"
"Who am I beyond who I think I am?"
"What lies beyond my fear?"

How do we trust what our hearts tell us? At first we can experience a dissonance between this new information and the ways we've thought of ourselves or how our culture wants us to be. As we keep on listening, we realize that what our hearts have to say rings true.

One of the effects of opening our hearts to ourselves is that we see how our patterns have affected us and those around us. These may show up in our relationships with ourselves, other people, or in the way we react to situations. This new vision causes us pain and dismay.

"I was appalled to see how my patterns of power and control had affected my relationship with my partner. It hurt me to see how much hurt I had inflicted on us both. This hurt forced me to look at myself and my behavior. I realized how much I loved my partner, and I knew that if I wanted to keep this relationship, I needed to live from my loving heart, and to let go of these patterns that came out of fear. I realized that my spiritual journey had led me to this clarity, yet it felt like I had jumped off a cliff into an abyss of hurt, regret and darkness." (Sally)

"I discovered that I was enabling unhealthy patterns within my family – with my partner and with my children. I was exhausted by the effort of keeping things peaceful on the surface while chaos was continually threatening to erupt underneath. When my youngest daughter was admitted to treatment for drug and alcohol abuse, I was forced to take responsibility for my part in what had become a dysfunctional family system. My spiritual practices had been preparing me

Our real journey in Life is interior. It is a matter of growth, deepening and an ever greater surrender to the creative action of love.

Thomas Merton[2]

for this 'fall', but I resisted it until I was pushed off the cliff of my old understanding, control, and fear into darkness. I found that in order to keep my heart open to my daughter, I had to enter into my own process of "recovery." (Suzanne)

At this point it is important to find someone with whom you can share your truth. This could be a good friend, a spiritual mentor, a counselor, or a group gathered to share spiritual stories. Telling your own story out loud to someone whose own life experiences allow them to truly hear you will make it more real for you and may give you courage to live out of your truth.

"By reflecting out loud to my spiritual director about my experiences, I am learning to use my voice to speak myself into being." (Eric)

"Once I had given voice to my own truth, I could no longer live what wasn't true for me." (Judi)

"Hearing similar questions and experiences from the women in my group gave me the courage to voice my own story. When I could hear the stories of others with compassion and I felt their compassion for me, I began to have compassion for myself." (Suzanne)

The word "compassion" in the above statement is important to consider since it heralds some significant developments. Compassion is unconditional empathy. It is the ability to accept and honor another's personhood without filtering their experiences through our own lenses. When we are compassionate we don't make assumptions about how others feel based on *our* feelings.

Some of us are naturally compassionate toward others and some of us learn compassion through opening our hearts. Either way, we begin with the ability to see ourselves with compassion. Unconditionally accepting our own personhood is about learning to love the truth in each of us.

"When I could look at myself with compassion, I realized that I was more loveable and trustworthy than I

ever thought I was. I fell in love with myself." (Sally)

"When I began to laugh at my foibles and the critical, overly-responsible voice in my head began to lose power, I knew that I had tapped into a well of compassion for my own self." (Suzanne)

It is in this process of beginning self-acceptance and self-trust that we feel a greater connection to our Source – Spirit, God, whatever we might wish to name it.

"I felt like I was on a honeymoon. I was basking in love. All my senses were alive and sensitive to every nuance of my spiritual experience." (Jack)

"I felt high as a kite. I had never felt so alive. My mind was crystal clear. I felt so loved and was so in love with Spirit." (Brian)

We bask in the sensations of this state of connection. We relish all of the spiritual tools we can find to enhance this new awareness.

"I was sitting in meditation when an image came to me of an old man whose eyes shone with compassion saying, 'It is the light of the heart that illumines the mind.' Needless to say, my heart was deeply touched. My first response was a deep awareness that my mind needed to listen to my heart -- that my heart was to be in charge. I felt a reorientation occur in me that focused my spiritual practice toward exploring the light in my heart." (Sally)

"I was on a personal retreat, sitting in the garden of the retreat center. A breeze came up and began to blow the leaves of the birch trees underneath which I was sitting. As the breeze touched my face, I felt an overwhelming sense of unconditional love and acceptance. I had the distinct impression that this love was coming from the feminine spirit of God. It felt as if this feminine presence loved me as I loved my children

Speak your truth.
Listen when others speak
theirs, too.
When you let go of fear,
you will learn to love
others,and you will let
them love you.
Do not be afraid of dying.
But do not be afraid to
live.
Ask yourself what that
means.
Open your heart to love,
for that is why you're here.
And know that you are,
and always have been
Onewith Me and all who
live.

   Melody Beattie₃

– deeply and totally. My heart opened to this love and all the possibility it held for me because I recognized it as a love I knew – that of mine for my children. My spiritual practice became more heart-centered after this experience." (Suzanne)

SELF-REFLECTION

OPENING THE HEART

Here are two spiritual practices focusing on opening the heart. You may want to choose one to incorporate into your own practice. If not, develop a ritual of your own around something that touches your heart, such as a piece of music, a work of art, an experience in nature, a poem, or essay.

"One of the tools I often use in my own spiritual practice is what Ron DelBene calls a "Breath Prayer",[3] I ask myself the question, "What is my heart's deepest desire at this time?" I usually have to ask the question more than once in order to get below the more mundane and practical needs that often surface first. When I have a word or phrase that resonates within my heart, I put it into a simple prayer that can be said in one short breath.

'To you, O God, I surrender this journey.'

(I came to this prayer when I had a great need and desire to let go of my own control over people, situations, and even over my spiritual journey with the Mystery I call God).

I keep the prayer close to my heart and mind and say it often. For example, I may say it before I arise in the morning and sleep at night, when I am walking, as I enter into silence, when I am sitting in the car at a red light or when a situation during the day calls the desire of my heart to mind. I keep a particular breath prayer until it feels like the desire has been met—which may mean weeks or months. I have found over time, that the prayer changes me and keeps my heart open to new ways of being and seeing." (Suzanne)

"One of my spiritual practices is to sit among the big trees in a state park close to my home. I take a beach chair and just go sit with the trees, looking at them, feeling their towering strength all around me, until I feel at peace. Then I listen with my heart to the silence, taking into the silence the rustle of a breeze through their branches, and the birdcalls. As I sit in the silence, I breathe as if I am breathing directly through my heart, allowing my heart to soften and my heart space to expand out to meet the trees. I am opening myself to whatever is deepening in me and connecting me with the Source of all. I may sit for an hour or more. When I feel complete, I write anything that may have come to me in my journal. Then I return home." (Sally)

Notes

Pilgrimage of the Soul

Notes

7

SENSING ENERGY

> *Energy is the substance of life, the unrelenting wellspring of pure
> possibility, escalating and undulating as in a great cosmic dance. . . . It
> unfolds amid movement, connection, and relationship, defying, from the
> scientific point of view, concrete description or definition, but evoking in
> the mystic primordial images of some great dancer dancing the world into
> being.*

Diarmuid O'Murchu[1]

As we move along in our spiritual journeys, we become more
aware of the subtle shifts in our own energy and the energy of
others, especially close family and friends. We sense others' changes
of mood, such as anxiety or excitement. We know when our own
energy level is high or low, or when our energy is scattered.
We begin to ask, "What is energy all about anyway?"

"My greatest awareness of energy came while I was sitting in my dark time. I remember thinking that this void might not be empty after all. It, perhaps, was full of energy that I could not perceive yet. If I thought about nature, I realized that when humans and animals are in the dark, they are usually in gestation. What if that were happening to me? If so, what was being gestated? As I sat with these questions, I began to be aware of the energy within me—the energy of my thoughts, my feelings, and how they were heavier than the energy of my meditations, which seemed so light." (Sally)

"Sitting in silence, learning to befriend the darkness, I began to feel connected to all the elements of creation that also often wait in silent darkness…the bulbs underground, the stones at the bottom of the riverbed, the caterpillar in its cocoon, the bear in its den of hibernation. While they wait, transformation is slowly taking place – energy is shifting and creating new forms. I felt a kinship with other structures of creation and began to wonder what form I would take when the darkness lifted. I felt energy stirring in places I had never felt it before, in my dreams, in my breath, in my creativity, in my soul. It seemed in some subtle, indescribable way that I was tapping into the energy of the Universe." (Suzanne)

All living organisms are energy systems. This idea has been accepted and used in non-Western cultures for centuries. This energy is expressed as *prana* in India, *chi* in China or *ki* in Japan. We humans are recognized as open energy systems, engaged in a continuous interaction with the energy of the environment in which we live. Light, air, oxygen, water, soil, plants, animals, minerals, and other persons directly influence our lives. [2]

Matter is simply dense energy that has a shape and form. Matter and energy (what scientists call particle and wave), body and spirit, are not two separate things. The human body is the material substance of our life force, spiritual energy.

We are composed of a mind with which we think and believe, an emotional nature with which we feel, a free will by which we make choices, and a physical body that enables us to live in the dimensions of time and space. Each of these is a manifestation of energy of increasing density. Our thought forms and beliefs are of denser energy than our subtle spirit; our emotions and will are of greater density than our thought forms; and our physical bodies are the densest form of human energy. All aspects of our being are forms enlivened by the same flow of life force energy. This flow of energy through all parts of us becomes apparent in the interaction between our emotions, bodies, and minds.

"I have had so much work stress, that my blood pressure has hit the roof, and I've been having chest pains. I guess I need to realize how much the stuff going on with my co-workers hurts me, and not continue to push it down, hoping it will go away. I feel that I have some spiritual purpose in my work there, so it has been hard to fully acknowledge the hurt." (Paula)

"I just returned from a family gathering for my grandmother's funeral. I was able to stay present to my own feelings and my own center. However, when I returned home, I became irritable and unable to sleep. I feel like my energy was depleted by having to cope with the toxic energy of my dysfunctional family and that I have to re-gather it again." (Geri)

How do we recognize spiritual energy? This is a subtle yet powerful energy that, at first, evokes an emotional response. We can feel touched to the point of tears, vulnerable, open, compassionate, and even momentarily disoriented.

"On a youth work camp project in Louisiana, where I was an adult leader, I spent one night in a small chapel pondering the economic inequities between the lives of the people in the African-American community in which I was working each day and the lives of the members of the wealthy

white church in which I was housed. As I wrestled with questions of injustice, bigotry, poverty and suffering, I felt a powerful presence calling me to be a bridge between the church and the world. I was brought to tears by the compassion that opened up within me and I also felt in awe of the power of this "call" and all that would change in my life if I embraced this spiritual experience. I walked around dazed for weeks, deeply aware that my whole life had been radically re-oriented." (Suzanne)

"One of my early spiritual experiences happened while I was working on a project for a spiritual class I was taking. One day as I was sitting thinking about this project, I got what I could only describe as a blast of energy that came in through the crown of my head, and my project was all laid out very clearly in my mind. As I completed the project, I was filled with awe, joy, and felt as high as a kite. During the next few days, I felt more open, and therefore more vulnerable. I felt compassion toward people I met, and a deep connection to animals and trees. I continued to feel high for weeks, and had great difficulty staying grounded and focused on the activities of daily life." (Sally)

This sense of joy, awe, and disorientation is often experienced as a sort of bliss, making it hard for us to stay connected to our lives. The tendency is to want to remain in this "blissed-out" state and to ignore our personal responsibility and accountability to our work, family and friends. It is crucial to find ways to ground this energy by staying present in our daily activities, as difficult as that may be. In our work we have seen people who have become depressed following peak spiritual experiences. They became so enraptured with the bliss that they were no longer present to their lives and gradually became numb, isolated and saddened. Staying grounded in our activities and relationships allows us to absorb the energy of the experience and to bring that energy into our lives.

What do we mean by "grounded" and how do we stay

there? Grounded means we are as fully present as possible in all our activities and relationships. It means being in the present moment as well – not projecting into the future nor dwelling on the euphoria of the peak experience. Being grounded helps us to integrate the energy that infuses us during spiritual experiences.

As we integrate the energy of spiritual experiences, we become a container for it. How do we learn to be a container for our spiritual energy? The first step is becoming aware of how we don't contain our energy. Spiritual energy opens us in every sense of the word and it will be channeled into whatever opening is available. This energy will intensify ego power, sexual attraction, creativity, addictions, devotion, service, or repression due to fear. One of the most common examples of this is falling in love with someone after a peak spiritual experience. When this happens our spiritual energy can be so luminous that we draw people to us and project our energy out onto them. We can sexualize that exchange of energy and call it love.

"At a spiritual retreat, I found myself attracted to a woman in my small group. In a short time, we were both enraptured with each other and felt our love was confirmed by the spiritual setting in which we had found each other. As our relationship intensified, we became engaged and thought we had the support and blessing of the entire spiritual retreat community and we wanted to be married in that setting. When the retreat community decided that we instead should celebrate our marriage with family and friends and in the spiritual context of our own hometowns, our relationship began to falter. Within weeks, we ended the engagement and were estranged from each other. Our fellow retreatants honored our feelings of anger, remorse and sadness, but refused to "take sides". In the end, I was able to acknowledge how my deep spiritual experience on this retreat had opened my heart to another vulnerable person. I had projected my longing and my bliss onto this woman without adequate time

for self-reflection in which to understand the awesomeness of
my own spiritual experience." (Matthew)

Another way we can dissipate our spiritual energy is to dive into some work of service and lose ourselves in the process.

"A profound spiritual experience called me into
working with refugees. I rode the energy to the point where
I found myself exhausted and burned out, and didn't have
anything else to give to the work. This was confusing to me
because I thought this what I was led to do. I needed to step
away and to examine my motivations for throwing myself into
this with such abandon. I needed to regain balance and discern
if the call was valid and if so, how I can live it in a balanced
way." (Joanna)

Some of our spiritual experiences are so awesome that we can retreat in fear and refuse to acknowledge the energy we felt. Or, we can dissipate our spiritual energy by judging ourselves undeserving of the experience.

"I was attending a workshop led by Trish, who was teaching
us spiritual healing. As she worked on Pat, a woman with
thyroid cancer, I realized that I could see what she was doing
inside Pat's body. I saw Trish place a triangle of golden energy
around Pat's thyroid gland. Trish asked me what I saw and
I told her. As she confirmed what I had seen, I became both
astounded and afraid of my vision. It was such an awesome
experience that I felt undeserving of the vision, and afraid
that somehow this experience might carry with it some huge
responsibility. Eventually, I came to see that this was simply
an experience of spiritual energy flowing through me, allowing
me to 'see' in a different way. It was no more nor less than
that." (Sally)

"My first experience with healing touch was in the
context of a spiritual retreat. We were asked to partner up
with another person, give a silent intention for help or healing
and then to gently lay hands on the person's head, shoulders

*and feet. After the exchange, my partner spoke in glowing
terms about the profound sense of healing she experienced
when I lay my hands on her. I was amazed, confused and
frightened. Though I, too, had felt "something" happen and
some energy flow through me to my partner, I was afraid
to acknowledge it. It felt like she was proclaiming me a
healer and I didn't want the responsibility carried by that
word. Later that evening, I was able to put my feelings into
perspective and recognize that I could be a conduit or channel
for what ever healing energy was coming from Spirit, without
being in any way the direct cause of a particular healing event.
If healing had happened that day for my partner, it was not
because of me, but merely through me, and it might or might
not happen again." (Suzanne)*

If we have a tendency toward addiction, we might
numb ourselves from our spiritual energy by anesthetizing
ourselves with drugs, alcohol, sex, work, food or shopping.

*"I came home from a retreat feeling high as a kite. I
wanted to sit in the back yard and have a glass of wine. One
glass seemed to help me to see the whole retreat experience
more clearly, so I had several more glasses of wine. Pretty soon
I had lost all of the good feeling from the retreat and just felt
numb. Over the next day or so, I found that I could not bring
back the insights that had seemed so apparent and important
for me." (Ron)*

We can scatter our spiritual energy by talking about an
experience too soon, before we have absorbed it and have words
for it, or by trying to explain it to others who don't understand.

*"I found that talking about my spiritual experiences
too soon, or with friends who didn't understand, was like
uncovering a bulb before it had a chance to sprout thus
endangering its growth process. Talking about my spiritual
experience before it had a chance to root and grow in me,
took all of the energy and power out of it; thus preventing*

the growth that those experiences might have given me."
(Suzanne)

Our egos love spiritual experiences. These experiences offer a way to see our selves as spiritually better than others.

"I felt as though my frequent experiences in
communicating with birds was something very special. It
wasn't long before I began to think that I was very special,
too, being able to do this thing that others were envious of.
A while later, I realized that the birds no longer came to me,
no matter how I tried to summon them. As I wondered what
had happened to my gift, I began to see how I had misused the
energy by making such an ego trip out of it. As I learned
to sit in my spiritual energy without allowing my ego to take
over, the birds began to visit me and communicate once again."
(Sally)

We have explored some of the ways we dissipate our spiritual energy, now, how do we contain it? The most basic way to contain our spiritual energy is with a daily spiritual practice. It is our practice that keeps our ego in check, that calms our anxiety, that steadies us during change, and that helps us put our excess energy into creative endeavors. Our daily practice is most beneficial to us when it becomes as routine as brushing our teeth. The quality of the experience is not the issue, it is the regularity with which we open ourselves to receiving spiritual energy that transforms us over time.

"My practice is to walk every morning and tune
myself in to creation and its spiritual energy." (Bret)

"I sit in silence every day with my cup of coffee and
look out the front window at the tall trees. While I sit I am
listening for the voices of soul and spirit." (Sara)

"Every morning, I sit with my journal and relax
into the vision of spirit holding me, just being aware of being
present and listening." (Sally)

*"After my morning shower, I sit and write about my
dreams, do a short spiritual reading, reflect and write in my
journal." (Suzanne)*

*"I begin my day with yoga postures to awaken my
energy and center my soul." (Dara)*

In addition to spiritual practice, there are a number of ways
to contain spiritual energy. Sharing with those who can validate or
help us to own our experiences can assist us in integrating spiritual
energy. Do you have relationships in your life that support your
spiritual awareness? Do you have a soul friend, or is there a group
of people with whom you can share your spiritual experiences and
questions. Do you have ways to express your creativity? Expressive
arts give us a way to record and give form to spiritual energy. Are
you able to set the boundaries that help to maintain balance in
your life? Setting boundaries can mean that you do not share your
spiritual experiences with people who will denigrate, or will not
respect them. Setting boundaries can also mean making time for all
of these activities.

There is a difference between containing our energy and
grasping, or holding on to, the energy that comes from spiritual
experiences. When we contain our energy, we allow it to flow
through us, using it to foster our relationships and work. When
we grasp at spiritual experiences to make them last or to repeat
themselves, we interfere with the natural flow of our energy. The
more that we can just allow spiritual experiences to flow through
our lives, the more we become grounded and spiritually deepened.

Some of us are very sensitive to our own energy and the
energy of others. We may have psychic abilities that enable us
to "read" others' energy to a high degree. These readings may be
registered emotionally, physically, with images, odors or sounds.
We can mistake such psychic gifts as the end of the journey rather
than part of a greater spiritual process. When we can place our
gifts within the context of the whole journey, we run less risk of
becoming stalled, side-tracked or empowering our egos.

"I have always been very 'psychic' and able to read others' energies and, to a great extent, be able to tell them about themselves. I could sense their feelings and see their energy. When I was young, because no one around me knew what I was talking about, I kept my abilities hidden. Then, in my thirties, I decided to see what I could do with my gift if I used it for healing work with those who felt they needed what I had to offer. I thought I knew what my spiritual journey was all about. But, as I became quite well known and in demand, it all turned into an ego trip. I gradually realized that there was much more to my spirituality than my psychic ability. I can see, now, how my ability to work with energy can be an important part, yet only a part, of my spiritual life."
(Georgia)

As we are developing the ability to read energy, we can confuse the energy we pick up from others with our own. Over time we learn to differentiate between the two. But, during this learning process, there are times when we are aware that others' energy has provoked in us an emotional response of fear, anxiety, or intimidation. When this happens, these people feel toxic to us and we want to avoid them. There are ways we can deflect such energy, ground it or clear our selves of it.

"A woman new to the state wanted to meet with me to talk about her vocation and job possibilities in our area. She had many stories to tell me of how she had been devalued and dismissed in her previous places of service. I offered some suggestions and ways to make contact with others who might help her get established in our region. After I left our meeting and was driving back to my office, I was suddenly overwhelmed with anxiety. I almost had to pull the car over because I was beginning to panic and felt very physically disoriented. I couldn't figure out what was happening. I wondered if I had eaten some bad food or something.

A few weeks later, I was reading a book about how toxic energy from another person can catch us unaware and that we can react violently to it. I immediately thought about my encounter with this woman and my unusual reaction afterward. From that time on, whenever I am in this woman's presence, I keep a good physical distance from her, I deflect her requests for any serious conversation to someone else and I clear my energy system by sweeping my hands over my body and directing the negative energy I get from her into the ground." (Suzanne)

"I worked with a colleague whose energy felt like a blow to my solar plexus whenever we were engaged in conversation. Interaction with her was an important part of my work, so I had to learn how to take care of myself. I learned to do several things to prepare myself each time before I met with her. I would take a few moments to acknowledge my own light, and to imagine a shield of light around me. Then while we were meeting, I would turn my body slightly so that her energy would not flow directly into the front of my body, and at the same time, I would imagine her energy going straight into the ground, not entering my energy field at all. Over time, these techniques became automatic, and I found I could hear her and interact with her without feeling affected by her energy." (Sally)

Working with a spiritual director or teacher who understands these phenomena helps you to integrate your experiences in a way that is meaningful for you. For many of us, psychic experiences come about as part of our growing spiritual awareness. It is helpful to remember that they are not the goal of the journey.

As we become more skilled and comfortable with sensing energy, our awareness expands with the understanding of our connection to the greater energies of the universe. We are part of the great cosmic dance of which O'Murchu speaks in the quote that opens this chapter. Our human energy, like cosmic energy "unfolds amid movement, connection and relationship". Awareness of our energy is part of the preparation for the shift of identity that lays before us on the spiritual journey.

SELF-REFLECTION

ENERGY AWARENESS EXERCISES

- Rub the palms of your hands together. Separate your hands by slowly and repeatedly moving them apart and then closer until you feel the "ball" of energy between them.
- With your palms facing your body, move your hands repeatedly farther away and closer until you can feel your energy field around your body.

Energy Clearing Technique

This is a effective technique to center yourself if you are in any kind of emotional turmoil, or if your mind is going ninety miles an hour, or if you have been around energy that feels bad or toxic to you. It can take only five to ten minutes.

Imagine that high above your head is a white vortex of energy—much like a gentle, white tornado. The point of this vortex comes down through the crown of your head and continues down along your spinal column. The upper, or wide, part of the vortex comes down around you and your energy field. It rotates clockwise, (left-to-right, if you were to look down on it.) It will move down through you and on into the ground. Your intention is that the vortex will clear energy that is no longer needed by you so that you can be centered.

Chakra meditation

The human energy system contains seven major energy centers called chakras. If you think about our life force (spiritual energy) as light, then these centers act as prisms that bend the light into colors (frequencies of energies) for use by a particular chakra. Each chakra has a location in the body and a purpose associated with it. (See Fig. 1 on the next page)

THE SEVEN MAJOR CHAKRAS[1]

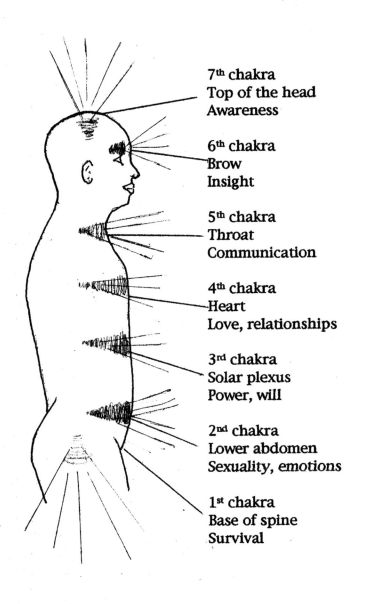

7th chakra
Top of the head
Awareness

6th chakra
Brow
Insight

5th chakra
Throat
Communication

4th chakra
Heart
Love, relationships

3rd chakra
Solar plexus
Power, will

2nd chakra
Lower abdomen
Sexuality, emotions

1st chakra
Base of spine
Survival

Figure 1

Sit in a comfortable position in a comfortable chair. Take your time with this meditation. In fact, you might want to record yourself saying it, giving yourself time between each step in order to become fully aware of each part of the experience. Then you can use the tape regularly to lead yourself into this meditation. Accept whatever images or sensation come to you during this process.

Take three deep breaths—with the first breath, allow your body to relax, releasing any tension and tightness. With the second breath, relax your emotions, again releasing any tension or tightness. With the third breath, relax your mind, not holding on to any thoughts—let them float by like bubbles.

Now bring your focus to your heart chakra in the center of your sternum, or breast bone. Imagine, that as you focus your awareness there, a flower appears and opens its petals. A color emerges from the center of the flower that flows in and out of the chakra, softening the center, opening it more deeply, and dissolving what is no longer needed by that chakra. Take all the time you need for this.

Then leave this chakra to continue clearing while you follow a beam of light down to your solar plexus chakra—about two inches above your navel. Again, as you focus on this chakra, imagine a flower appearing and opening. A color emerges from its center, flowing through the center, softening it, opening it more deeply, and dissolving whatever is no longer needed.

Again, leave that center to continue its work, and follow the beam of light down to your sacral center about two inches below your navel. As you focus your attention on this chakra, a flower opens, and a color emerges from its center. The color flows through the center, softening it and dissolving whatever is no longer needed.

Leave this chakra to follow the beam of light to your base chakra just below your pubic bone. This is the chakra that faces downward toward the Earth. Imagine a flower opening and a color emerging from its center. The color softens and opens the center more deeply, and dissolves whatever is no longer needed.

As you leave this center, follow the beam of light back up through the sacral, solar plexus, and heart charkas, and then up to the center at your throat—just at the notch between your collarbones. Again, imagine that a flower opens, and a color emerges. The color flows through the flower, softening and opening the chakra, and dissolving anything that is no longer needed.

Leaving this chakra, follow the beam of light up to the chakra between your eyebrows. Again, imagine a flower opening and a light emerging and flowing through the center which softens and opens the chakra more deeply, and dissolves whatever is no longer needed.

Leaving this chakra, follow the beam of light up to the crown chakra at the top of your head. Now, imagine a white light flowing into you through this crown chakra. Imagine that it swirls down through you as if it were a liquid light. The light flows through each of the charkas, and throughout all of your energy system. It flows throughout your mental, emotional systems, and through every cell in your body. Take all the time you need with this light so that it can dissolve all that is no longer needed in each of those areas.

When this cleansing and balancing process with the light has subsided and feels complete, return your focus to your crown chakra, and imagine a rainbow of color flowing into you through this chakra. This is a rainbow of nourishing energy that will flow through your system in the same way as the white light. Each color is of a frequency of energy that is used by various aspects of you. Each chakra, your mental and emotional systems, and your physical body will take what it needs from the rainbow. Again, take your time with this until it subsides or feels complete. Then rest in this completeness as long as you like.

When you are ready, return your attention to your charkas. Starting with the base chakra, close each one by imagining that the flowers are closing for the night—but close them only three-quarters closed. It is important not to be out in the world wide open as we are like vacuum cleaners and will pick up too much of others' energy. Nor do we want the charkas closed tight, because that will block our energy.

Pilgrimage of the Soul

Notes

Notes

Crossing the Second Threshold

I am an Spiritual Human Being

I AM A SPIRITUAL HUMAN BEING

104

Pilgrimage of the Soul

8

BEING PRESENT

"To discover the mystery of the ordinary, it is not enough to go through the motions of rising, walking, eating, resting, as we have done every day of our life. Going through the motions mechanically and mindlessly is counterproductive. What is helpful is to be gently, attentively present to the full reality of our human experience here and now. Then these ordinary happenings can become vehicles that carry us towards the mystery of God [Spirit].

Charles Cummings[1]

" I'm scared. To plunge more deeply into this path now means really trusting that this process will take me where I'm supposed to go. I don't know if I'm ready for that kind of trust. It means that I'll have to open myself more, and I don't know if I can be my own genuine self all of the time. I'm so used to choosing which parts of myself I'll reveal to which person. It's become such a habit. Yet, I know how much I feel connected to God when I meditate, and I really do want more of that connection all of the time. I know there is really no choice but to go deeper into my

*spirituality. I know that somewhere in there, the richness
of my soul lies waiting."(George)*

Remember George, from the Introduction, who felt trapped
and disillusioned on the fast track? Well, as he began paying attention
to his feelings, he realized how much he needed to slow down. This
awareness frightened him, because he knew that if he took the time
to see what his discomfort was all about, he would be entering an
unknown territory in himself. He was no less fearful about what
his slowing down might mean in his employment. But, he was also
afraid *not* to explore what was going on within him.

In spite of his fears, he plunged into the inner work, and asked
for and received accommodations from his employer. He stepped
down into a less demanding position, one that he had done before
and that didn't require so much of his energy. He found himself
a mentor to help him, a friend who had earlier found himself in
a similar situation and was moving through it. George began his
spiritual deepening.

Now, he found himself on a new threshold. He could see
the ways that he still struggled with his need for control in his life,
and, at the same time, knew that his spiritual path was leading him
beyond that kind of control.

He was startlingly aware of how much he was not really present
to either himself or his life. In many ways, he just went mindlessly
through the motions of daily activities. Going unconscious was like
a slippery slope to him. It had helped him survive his childhood,
and he had become very good at it. He often didn't know he wasn't
present until he was centered again and then could feel the difference.
But, later, his clarity would slip away; he knew something wasn't
quite right, but couldn't name it.

*"It's as though, when I'm not present, I forget
what presence is, or how to get there. Then, I read an
inspiring poem, or meditate, and I'm present again, and*

I realize that I've been absent—running on automatic pilot."(George)

He could see that his spiritual practice was helping him recognize the difference between being present and being absent. He also realized that he still kept parts of himself hidden from others. He still had lingering doubts that he was really acceptable if he wasn't the person that everyone expected him to be.

We find ourselves stepping through the second Threshold when we make the conscious commitment to a deeper, more permanent shift from our ego driven values, beliefs and control, to the deeper values of presence, authenticity, and intentional choices. This conscious shift moves us irrevocably toward our souls, where we know ourselves to be undivided and at one with our Source. As we claim our spiritual values, we gradually become self-identified as a human being beyond our ego power and control. Our souls, and Source, challenge us to move consciously from a human *doing* to a human *being*.

Our ego consciousness is not accustomed to being in the present, but rather in memories of our past and in our hopes for the future. In this new choice, we are being asked to move beyond our egos and to reclaim our capability of being "present to the present".

Many of us may not be ready for this challenge the first time it comes around. But, rest assured, there will be other opportunities to make this conscious choice as your soul nudges you into alignment with your Source.

One way we claim our ability to be present is by paying attention to our emerging sense of wholeness, noticing those aspects of our lives that nurture that sense, as well as those aspects that evoke our inner separation into compartments.

"An image of wholeness, for me, is a tree.
Whatever the size of the tree, it has roots, trunk,
branches, and some sort of leaf. No matter what stage of

growth it is in, it is always whole." (Suzanne)

"If one looks long enough at almost anything, looks with absolute attention at a flower, a stone, the bark of a tree, grass, snow, a cloud, something like revelation takes place. Something is 'given' and perhaps that something is always a reality outside the self." May Sarton [2]

"One of the ways I notice how I get separated inside is when I perceive that something is "not right" with the person I'm with at the moment. If I start to think that somehow I am responsible for the other person's feelings, and that I have to "fix" whatever is going on, then I feel out of balance myself and know that I'm compartmentalizing myself." (Sally)

Another way we reclaim our ability to be present is when we realize that we are ordinary people. We are never fully present when we live out of the ego belief that we are special. That "specialness" separates us from others, mirroring our own internal patterns of separation.

"My first awareness of not being special came when I was serving communion after being ordained. As each person came up to receive the bread and wine, I realized that each one had had some experience of brokenness in their life—some failure, grief, disappointment, or loss of dreams. Despite outward appearances of stability and status, they were all the same in their brokenness. And I was no different. We were all at the same table, all acceptable and accepted." (Suzanne)

The most essential way of reclaiming being fully present is by engaging in an ongoing spiritual practice. This may be the one time we actually practice being present without external distraction. In our spiritual practice, we learn to create a state of active attention in which we are relaxed yet alert. We accept *whatever is* moment to moment. Here we slip beyond time, space, and form—everything dissolves into pure awareness. We are not separate from anything. These experiences of pure awareness grace us with glimpses of the realm of our souls, and we carry back into everyday life our enhanced capacity to be present to ourselves and others.

Spiritual practice becomes more crucial at this stage of spiritual development, because it grounds our spiritual energies in presence. We have learned how to connect with our Source and to allow that grace to run through us. But, unless we deliberately channel that energy into being present—conscious--our egos, in their ongoing dance for power, will co-opt those higher frequencies of energy to strengthen ego control. This has the result of strengthening the very patterns we are trying to dis-empower and release. The ego has a large stake in us remaining unconscious and functioning on "automatic pilot." It keeps our world restricted, controlled, and safe for the ego.

Old habits are like slipping into comfortable old slippers. Being unconscious is like that, too. It takes no effort. Yet, it can leave us exhausted, lethargic, listless, and with a sense of futility. The reason for this is because we're keeping our spiritual life at arms' length by hiding behind the busyness of life and work.

The remedy for this state is a renewed commitment to stay present and to value the choices that we have made.

"I decided to stay at home with my two children after they were born. At first I chafed against the decision because I felt that my days were full of nothing important (like my former work as a teacher.) Gradually, I began to understand that being fully present to my young children was the most important work I could do at this time in my life. I embraced my choice and began to take joy in the rhythm of daily life as a mother." (Suzanne)

"I think we need more of the wordless in our lives. We need more stillness, more of a sense of wonder, a feeling for the mystery of life. We need more love, more silence, more deep listening, more deep giving."
Ben Okri[3]

Choosing to be present is overcoming the inertia of apathy.

"My counseling and spiritual direction work with clients is different from anything I have done before. Previously, I would take a position for a year or two or three, and when I had learned it, I would move on to something else, even if it were in the same institution. In hindsight, I know that it was a manifestation of my internal yearning and restlessness. Since I moved into this work with clients, I have to stay put. It is work I love, but I sometimes find myself feeling the old familiar restlessness to move on. Yet, there is nothing else to move on to. In order not to slide down into that familiar pattern of unconsciousness, I reclaim the value of what I am doing, and make a renewed commitment to being present. As I stay present, I can see that my recurrent restlessness happens before each internal shift I make into more depth." (Sally)

Choosing to be present is overcoming the inertia of apathy. It is the act of choosing to give meaning to one's life, by giving our full attention to whatever it is that we are engaged in, no matter the circumstances. It is the willingness to "stay put" and go deeper. Meaning doesn't just appear in our lives. We have to give life meaning by the choices we make and the genuine attention we put into the living of those choices.

"It took me quite a long time to understand that any aspect of my life could be meaningful if I approached it whole-heartedly.
It was as if I expected whatever I was doing to 'give' me whatever meaning it held. I looked to friends to give me meaning, and to relationships to fulfill me. It was all about someone or something outside of myself 'giving' to me. Of course, I was doing all that I could on my part—everything except being fully present. Once I began to learn what 'being present' meant, I found that I was the source of meaning in my life, simply by being fully present." (Alan)

One of the fruits of presence is *detachment*—perceiving without wanting to own, collect, or to possess. Acquisitiveness, the ego's need to acquire objects, people, and knowledge, is a large part of our conditioning in our materialistic culture. We see in every day life how peoples' collections of objects can be viewed on the mainstream television, how parent's can hold captive their children, or how people in power acquire knowledge and withhold it from their constituency.

In detachment, it isn't that we no longer care about what we have, or the people in our lives, or what we know, but rather we are free of the burden of having to possess them. We can have, know and love with our full attention and with reverence.

To love without
taking possession;
To act without
appropriating;
To excel without
standing over;
This is called the
inward mysterious
power
Of those who live
according to the Tao.
Lao Tzu[4]

SELF-REFLECTION

WALKING MEDITATION

"When you practice walking meditation, you go for a stroll. You have no purpose or direction in space or time. The purpose of walking meditation is walking meditation itself. Going is important, not arriving. Walking meditation is not a means to an end; it is an end. Each step is life; each step is peace and joy. That is why we don't have to hurry. That is why we slow down. We seem to move forward, but we don't go anywhere; we are not being drawn by a goal. Thus we smile while we are walking."

Thich Nhat Hanh[5]

Find a place and set aside a time to walk. Walk with no destination or goal. As you walk be aware of how your feet touch the earth, the way your legs feel as you walk, the posture of your back, the movement of your arms, your breathing, and the position of your head. Now, bring your senses into focus; is there a breeze? What colors and textures do you see? Are there odors? What do you hear? Be aware of what your senses bring to you in each moment.

After you have walked for a while, notice what feelings, worries, desires, and thoughts you are holding in your mind. Then, focusing on your breathing, with each exhalation let thoughts, worries, and desires float out on your breath.

Then, return to what your senses are inviting you to see, hear, smell in the present, and continue to walk for the pure joy of walking. Be present to each step and each moment.

Walking Meditation

Take my hand.
We will walk.
We will only walk.
We will enjoy our walk
Without thinking of arriving anywhere.
Walk peacefully.
Walk happily.
Our walk is a peace walk.
Our walk is a happiness walk.
Then we learn
that there is no peace walk;
that peace is the walk;
that there is no happiness walk;
that happiness is the walk.
We walk for ourselves.
We walk for everyone always hand in hand.
Walk and touch peace every moment.
Walk and touch happiness every moment.
Each step brings a fresh breeze.
Each step makes a flower bloom under our feet.
Kiss the Earth with your feet.
Print on Earth your love and happiness.
Earth will be safe when we feel in us enough safety.
May your walk be of peace,
and your spiritual direction practice point toward peace.

Thich Nhat Hanh[6]

Pilgrimage of the Soul

Notes

Notes

Pilgrimage of the Soul

Notes

9

BECOMING AUTHENTIC

*"Where we do sense our soul…is in our
discernment of our individuality – the fact that from
conception to birth we are the same person, a person
distinct from all other. The soul is the final locus
of our individuality. Situated as it were behind the
senses, it sees through the eyes without being seen, hears
through the ears without itself being heard. Similarly
it lies deeper than the mind. If we equate the mind
with the stream of consciousness, the soul is the source
of this stream."*

Huston Smith[1]

Becoming authentic is not about leaving our humanness behind. It is about offering our humanness in its most genuine form as a vehicle through which our soul finds expression. So, what does it mean to be authentic? What does it feel like? How does my authenticity impact others? How does it impact me?

*"For me, authenticity is letting others know my
experience and my perceptions." (Suzanne)*

*"Authenticity is about becoming transparent. It's
about allowing others to see and know what motivates me,
what I love, what I'm afraid of, what I'm passionate about.
It's about not hiding my deeper feelings." (Sally)*

Becoming authentic is not about leaving our humanness behind. It is about offering our humanness in its most genuine form as a vehicle through which our soul finds expression. So, what does it mean to be authentic? What does it feel like? How does my authenticity impact others? How does it impact me?

"Authenticity is about being courageous enough to allow myself to be open and vulnerable so that I can voice my own truth." (Steven)

An important part of becoming authentic is examining your motivations. Why do you behave in a certain way in order to please someone else, when your inner voice tells you to behave differently? Why are you silent when you have something to say? Why do you doubt your own perceptions in the face of others' views? Why are you engaged in a spiritual journey?

We bring into our spirituality the same expectations and motivations that we carry in the rest of our lives. Most of us enter into an experience because we want some personal benefit and ego gratification out of it. What is important here is that we become honest with ourselves about our motivations. Let us examine some of these motivations.

I WILL BE SAFE FROM SUFFERING

We all want to be free of pain and suffering. We try to avoid it through our addictions to work, relationships, substances, material goods, gambling, perfection, and control. We tend to believe that our spirituality will deliver us from having to look deeply and honestly at ourselves. However, spiritual practice and enlightenment will not help us to avoid that work. That is the human effort that we have to supply. There is a difference between spirituality and the human need to feel better. It is our human nature to believe that the closer we get to God or enlightenment the more we will be protected from pain and suffering. Yet, in reality, life is full of suffering and our spirituality will not necessarily make us feel better. In fact, it may make us more sensitive to suffering.

We just have a hard time accepting that fact. Why do we think we should be set apart and sheltered from distress? Because our egos want us to be special. Part of being authentic is learning to accept life as it is in any moment, not how we wish it to be.

"The real reason I wanted a spiritual teacher was to be rescued from the dark night I was experiencing. I felt like who I had known myself to be was being scraped away. I felt raw. All I could think about was the need for a teacher. I didn't think I could be in this state any longer. For a while, this teacher and his system of meditation helped. I could take on the identity of an abayassi – a disciple- in which I didn't have to know anything else about myself. But at the same time, the meditation practice opened my heart in new ways that allowed the rawness to resurface. This time it felt like an invitation to return home to it. I felt incomplete without it. One day, as I was sitting in the rawness, I felt myself shift through it into Peace. The rawness never returned." (Sally)

"I want a spiritual practice that brings me close to God so that I can be peaceful, so I can love people that I don't like, so I can forgive myself for not being good enough." (Elane)

I WILL BE ACKNOWLEDGED AND LOVED

The human need to be loved is certainly a powerful force. If we felt unloved growing up, we often feel that we don't deserve love as an adult, yet we crave it. We may also feel that we must earn love, and a spiritual path is one way to make love happen.

"Because I always wanted people to like me, I thought that if I became peaceful and loving through my spiritual practice that people would recognize my spiritual depth and would love me back." (Betty)

> *"I want to do my meditation practice so well that my teacher will acknowledge me. When he acknowledges me, I feel loved." (Daren)*
>
> *"If I could work hard enough to get to that place of union with God, nothing could separate me from being loved." (Trudy)*
>
> *"Good works will earn my place in heaven." (Bobby)*

Part of being authentic is learning to accept life as it is in any moment, not how we wish it to be.

To be authentic means that we question our un-worthiness and our need to earn love and begin to accept the possibility that we are loveable just as we are. This may entail a period of emotional work in which we examine where that need to earn love came from and what is needed for healing.

What we have yet to recognize is that Love is all around and in us. We don't have to earn it or ration it. Love flows through us as spiritual energy. We can only block Love. We block Love by feeling that we don't deserve it or can't have it. We also block Love by having to be "special" and be acknowledged for being extraordinary even in our spiritual practice.

I WILL GAIN SPIRITUAL POWER AND RECOGNITION

We recognize in others what we desire for ourselves, and as a result, are drawn to those who have spiritual qualities and behaviors we want to emulate. Receiving attention from these people can be very seductive. The ego wants to claim all possible adulation and we can come to rely on admiration for validation of our self worth. The risk here is that we will use our spiritual path primarily to acquire recognition, thereby jeopardizing the integrity of our spiritual growth.

This motivation arises out of our need to be seen as people of worth. It is based on the illusions of "I am what I do" and "I am what I have." If these illusions have not been dispelled then we carry them into our spirituality. Authenticity here means that we have to consider that we are more than what we do and what we have.

We have to realize that positions of power and possessions are only temporary satisfactions to our underlying yearning.

"When I was young and idealistic, I had a sincere desire to change the world in whatever work I did. But as time went on, I got caught up in meeting my own expectations that were way too high, and in being concerned about what others thought of me. As I look back on that time now, I can see what a strong motivation the opinions of others became for me as I tried to fashion myself in the image of who they thought I was." (Suzanne)

I WILL HAVE MORE CONTROL OF MY LIFE

We often have the belief that as we gain more spiritual awareness we will also gain a bigger arena of control. Our egos tell us that we will transcend the ordinariness of our lives and live in a place of enlightenment where we won't have mundane concerns. Yet, we want an enlightenment that we can control – one that meets our expectations. In reality the spiritual journey is often uneventful.

"Spiritual oneness will allow me to transcend and control my habits, weaknesses, and compulsions." (Paul)

"Following a spiritual path will enable me to move to a higher plane, where ordinary life will not control me." (Jackie)

"The structure of my spiritual practice gave me a way to be in control. I sat in prayer an hour each morning and evening, I read inspirational books. I went to church each week, I did all these things religiously and neglected the rest of my life including my relationships with my husband and children. These areas of my life were often unpredictable and I felt that I could do nothing to control them." (Elizabeth)

What we have yet to recognize is that Love is all around us and in us. We don't have to earn it or ration it.

"I felt very disappointed when my spiritual experiences changed so that I wasn't having all the highs that I found so affirming and rewarding. At first, I thought I was doing something wrong, but then, I realized that this is the nature of the spiritual journey." (Marina)

It is an illusion to think that we can transcend the ordinary. Because we are human we cannot live on a purely spiritual plane. Our everyday life is the ground upon which we practice our spiritual awareness. We express it daily in our relationships with loved ones, friends, co-workers and acquaintances and in our work. We see the affects of our awareness on ourselves and others. We have to come to understand that it is in the ordinary that we do the work of becoming authentic.

I WILL DISCOVER THE PURPOSE OF MY LIFE

We like to think that purpose will descend on us – that someday we will realize our mission in life. Many of us may have a sense of preparation – of being made ready for the doing of some great work. The good news about striving to find our purpose is that it keeps us seeking and walking our path. The down side is that our egos are still asking to be lifted out of our mundane existence. Purpose does not descend on us from Heaven. Instead we have to become attentive to life in order to imbue it with purpose. The more attentive we are the more purposeful and authentic we become. Attentiveness helps us see into the heart of things, including into ourselves.

"I must be here for some purpose beyond what I am doing now." (Jerry)

"My spiritual practice will lead me to the ways in which I can alleviate the suffering of others." (Aileen)

"I've had this ordinary life, and I don't feel that

I've done anything special. I keep on wondering what
I will be when I grow up. So, I've taken up a spiritual
practice to get the answer." (Kathie)

"I've begun a spiritual practice to make my life more
fulfilling." (Jerome)

As we move into more of our authenticity we see how these motivations influence us. We begin to question and de-construct them, to look beyond them to see what is really calling us. We settle in to accepting the idea that what motivated us into this spiritual journey may not be what is keeping us there. We are pulled more and more into alignment with the truth of our soul and treasure being there.

"I realize that I stay on my spiritual path because
I value my authenticity and the feeling of "rightness" it
brings me." (Aaron)

"I love that what is going on inside me is what
I present to the world. Authenticity has become a core
value for me and my spiritual practice keeps me attuned
to that value." (Marilyn)

"My spiritual journey is giving me the courage
to know and speak my own truth – what a liberating
experience!" (Diane)

Coming into our own authenticity allows us to become aware of how others' authenticity may be expressed differently from our own, and to realize that authenticity is simply each person becoming more fully themselves.

SELF-REFLECTION

> *"Becoming aware of our motivations for seeking enlightenment and pursuing the spiritual path is part of genuine and uncompromised spiritual work. Awareness creates the possibility of not being a slave to those motivations, not mechanically acting in egocentric ways while sincerely believing that one's intentions are holy and selfless. Knowing our impure motivations for enlightenment makes us more real, humbles us, brings us closer to ourselves and to our own suffering, and therefore to the suffering of others."*
>
> Mariana Caplan[2]

Here are some questions to consider during your times of reflection:

1. Over the next few weeks, give some thought to your own motivations for being on your spiritual path.
Do any of the motivation statements we've looked at in this chapter strike a chord with you?

For instance, are you engaged in this spiritual journey to:
- seek safety from suffering?
- earn love and acknowledgment?
- gain spiritual power?
- have more control of your life?
- have the purpose of your life revealed?

If none of these apply, what are your motivations?

2. Once we are on a spiritual path, we become more aware of ourselves and the ways that Spirit moves in our lives. We cannot become less aware. As a result, our motivations for continuing on the spiritual path frequently change. We may have started a spiritual journey to relieve some suffering, but later, find that our spiritual experiences deepen us in ways that make life more meaningful, and our earlier motivation is no longer what sustains us. How have your motivations changed?

3. What does it mean to you to be genuine or authentic?

Offer some gesture of gratitude for your increased awareness of the movement of Spirit in your life, such as bowing, opening your arms to acknowledge your Source, or placing your hands over your heart.

Pilgrimage of the Soul

Notes

*Our everyday,
ordinary life is the
ground upon which
we live out our
spiritual awareness*

Notes

Pilgrimage of the Soul

Notes

10

MAKING INTENTIONAL CHOICES

"When you're learning to face the path…every choice is worth your while."

Emily Saliers[1]

"I had this illusion that God should be enough for me. I felt that that relationship promised peace and happiness. But I wasn't peaceful or happy. My individual relationships with people weren't enough either. So, I finally figured out that my peace and happiness was up to me. While that didn't leave out God or people, it just meant that I could choose to be happy or not. I realized that it was a decision I could consciously make every day." (Darien)

Once we experience our authenticity as the truth of our soul, we start making intentional choices that foster a more genuine and truthful life. In a very real way, the choices we make from each new position of genuineness build and expand on our authenticity.

"Because at times I felt out of control in myself, I tried to control those around me. I wanted them to be how I wanted them to be. As I learned more about the feelings behind "going out of control" I was able to see how I was imposing control on those I loved. Accepting my own "stuff" allowed me to accept others just the way they were. I had to intentionally practice owning my own feelings and behavior, and to not act out of those feelings toward others." (Richard)

"I finally made the decision to tell my mother to not take so much responsibility for my life. I told her that I have my own path to walk and that I alone am responsible for my sobriety. I know that I have to do this for myself and not for her. I have to accept my addiction and the choices that I make about it." (Kayla)

Part of spiritual growth is bringing the capacity for choice into our consciousness. This requires intention and action. Intention means turning in the direction you want to go with some plan in mind. Intention implies a deliberate focusing of the mind toward a goal. Some intentions are tangible, such as cleaning the pantry. Others are more subtle, such as desiring to live without bitterness or resentment. Yet, intention alone is not enough. We must support our intention with our will by taking action. For example, if you want to live without resentment, what are the steps you must take to free yourself? The point, here, is that you must take the steps— merely intending to be free of resentment is not enough to liberate you. The same is true when we intend to do a spiritual practice. Practice calls for our active participation.

"I remember a turning point in deliberately making a choice to listen to someone with my heart instead of my head. I didn't like this person – someone I worked with. I had a difficult time with her, so I

*finally decided to ask myself, "What is she really saying?"
Trying to listen with my heart helped me learn that I
didn't have to say anything, respond in any particular
way – I just had to open my heart and listen. After
that I practiced just staying in my heart and listening,
instead of trying to think of my response before the
person finished talking." (Sally)*

*"A time of silence in the morning, even a very
short time, means starting my day by paying attention.
This practice sets my intention to be present to the
Source or God and frames the course of my day. My
day is usually filled with 'doing', and I find I have to
be deliberate about creating these times for just 'being'."
(Suzanne)*

*"I find that unless I create opportunities for
creative endeavors, they just don't happen. I schedule
time each week to pursue some creative project.
Sometimes it's difficult, yet as I practice doing this, I
find that it becomes more important and nourishing to
me." (Bev)*

Some of us may think that the spiritual path is about relinquishing our will, but instead it is about aligning our human will with our soul and its spiritual Source. Our will is usually at the beck and call of our ego as it strives for power. But, our spiritual Source is not about power. For a while, for some of us a long while, we engage in an ongoing dance where ego and soul try to move in harmony while both struggle to lead. During our spiritual journey, our ego eventually yields to our capacity to serve a higher purpose.

How do we know when we are aligned with our spiritual source? We engage in a process of discernment that helps us to attend to the subtleties of spirit.

DISCERNING THE SUBTLETIES OF SPIRIT:

Listening

Part of spiritual growth is bringing the capacity for choice into our consciousness.

"To listen to my soul means that I have to be solitary for periods of time. Sometimes I work in the yard, or take a hike, or just sit by the water for a little while. I just center myself and ask, 'What is it that my soul may be saying?' I don't expect a direct answer, and just being mindful of my soul becomes enough. Some time later I may get an insight or information that seems to guide me along my journey." (Sally)

"Paying attention to my dreams is one way I listen to my soul. I have learned to trust that God speaks to me in my dreams through images, sensations and emotions. Often, my dreams confirm a decision I make or bring insight to one that needs to be made. Dreams also point out places in need of healing or show me how healing is taking place. I find my dreams to be a deep source of connection to my soul and to my Source." (Suzanne)

"Journaling helps me to sort out my voice from all the other demanding voices in my life. It enables me to identify the 'shoulds' and 'oughts' that I hear from my ego and to listen to the voice of my soul and its longing." (Irene)

Waiting

"For me, much of the spiritual journey is about waiting and allowing Spirit to work in my life. It is about allowing my soul to unfold each day and take me where I need and want to go. This unfolding is a process that takes time and doesn't always proceed at the pace of 'ordinary' time." (Suzanne)

"I recently found a lump in my breast, and found myself waiting—waiting for tests to get scheduled, to be performed, to be given results. In the midst of it all, I thought, 'What if I think of this waiting as just a part of my spiritual path? What if I can just be centered in Spirit, and let all of this unfold? Just asking myself these questions served to center me, and I found I was peaceful about this medical process. (Eileen)

"Listening to my soul teaches me a lot about patience. I feel that I'm always waiting to see or hear what will come into my awareness. My ego always is looking to the future, and it is easy to become intolerant of the wait. Waiting requires me to be in the present moment only, and when I can do this, waiting becomes a centering exercise that places me in my soul". (Sally)

Moving from head to heart

"When I find myself waking up in the middle of the night with my mind full of things to figure out, I know that I am out of balance. I have learned that when my head is in control, I am more fearful, anxious and stressed. When I let my heart lead me and trust in those more intuitive and less analytical ways of knowing, I find that I am more in touch with my deepest self and with God. I can do all sorts of problem solving with my head, but if my heart is not beating in agreement, then the solution is not in line with my authentic self and will not be good for me." (Janice)

"Listening and waiting come from opening my heart to my soul. My head is full of disbelief and judgments, but my heart is full of compassion and openness. So, my work becomes that of shifting into my heart when communicating with my soul." (Kathleen)

Feelings

"It has taken me some time to know that my feelings are valid and need to be honored. That does not mean that I need to act on every feeling I have, but it does mean that I need to pay attention to my feelings because they offer insights and guides for the path ahead, whether it be in my relationships with others, with self or with my Source." (Suzanne)

"My feelings give me so much information—about people and situations around me. They also tell me about my inner world—when I am in tune with my soul or when I am following my ego. When I am in tune with my soul I feel a vast clarity inside, as if the whole universe is available to me. When my ego is in charge, I feel constricted, anxious, and wanting to be in control." (Sally)

Perception

" I am always looking for what is behind or underneath something…for the meaning behind the word, action, feeling, or experience. This perception has been with me since I was a child, but I did not see it as a blessing until I realized that if it helps me to listen to my own inner voice and to see Spirit working in all things."(Sally)

"When I am listening to my soul, my perception seems to shift to a place beyond my human self. I find myself seeking and opening to the deeper truths behind what is already apparent to me. I find myself asking, 'What is the greater reality here? 'What is the deeper perspective?' (Suzanne)

Inner Compass

"When I am in tune with the Source of my being, it feels like my inner compass is pointing true North. I am at peace, content, mindful of the richness

of the present moment and able to trust that all will be well." (Bobbi)

"As I am learning to listen and follow my soul, it becomes both my guiding light and the means to following the light. All I need seems to be contained in my soul. As I stay attuned with it, the rest of my life unfolds in ways that become increasingly aligned with my soul." (Eric)

As we learn to discern the messages of our soul, choices become easier, in a way. A good rule of thumb is to sleep on the choice and see how you feel the next day. Choices made from our soul leave us energized, enlivened and consoled. Choices made from our egos leave us depleted of energy and disheartened. Dancing with the question, "Am I going to live from a place of power or of love?" we become aware of how our choices will support one or the other. When our choices leave us enlivened it is important to trust that choice, even when circumstances or people might oppose it.

Mystery penetrated every aspect of my life with you, Dvine Secret. I cannot know or understand where the call to be yours will take me. I do not need to know even though I want to know. All that is required is that I trust you with my life. Wrap your love around me so completely that I will readily give you my "yes."

Joyce Rupp [3]

The Examen makes us aware of moments that at first we might easily pass by as insignificant, moments that ultimately can give direction for our lives

Dennis Linn, et al[2]"

SELF-REFLECTION

THE EXAMINATION OF CONSCIOUSNESS— THE EXAMEN

The Examen is a spiritual practice, originating with St. Ignatius of Loyola. Is to be done on a daily basis so that you can begin to notice emerging patterns. These will point to decisions you need to make about an action to take, a path to follow, or something that needs to be confronted and released.

Choose one form of the following questions to ask yourself at a consistent time each day--perhaps at the end of the day, or during the transition from work to home. Keep track of your responses in a journal. Begin to notice any emerging patterns. If a particular behavior, work situation, or relationship is continually life-draining, what can you do to change it? Take note of the life-giving situations, attitudes or relationships. How can you make these things more prominent in your life? Do they point toward a direction in which you need to move?

Sit quietly, center yourself, and ask yourself the following questions:

When did I feel most alive today?

When did I feel the life draining out of me?

Other ways to ask these questions:

When today did I have the greatest sense of belonging to myself, others, God (Spirit), and the universe?

When did I have the least sense of belonging?

For what moment today am I most grateful?

For what moment today am I least grateful?

Notes

Pilgrimage of the Soul

Notes

Notes

Crossing the Third Threshold

Beyond "I"

BEYOND "I"

11

TRANSFORMING THE EGO

*"The border crossing to the Ground of
Being, long closed by edict of the ego, is opened."*
Kathleen Dowling Singh[1]

*"One day, I became aware of having no more
questions, or perhaps it is that I no longer need answers.
I've settled somewhere in my depths where I am no
longer seeking, striving, and searching for answers.
In addition, I have no fear. All the fears of not being
good enough, of not knowing enough, of not doing this
journey in the "right" way, of not being safe enough, of
not being loved enough, are dissolving somehow. I feel
as though there has been a state of grace in me, at my
core, that I'm only now realizing. It is a new state of
being to me. I feel soul-filled. I have a sense of freedom.
I feel deeper and larger than all of my strivings. I feel
as though this old ego of mine, which in so many ways
has served me well, no longer defines me in any way.*

Of course, I do know that my ego hasn't vanished, and that I probably will always 'know' how to be ego-driven. But hopefully, I will make choices that will support this newly recognized state of being.

With this shift in me has come a new perspective. There is no more questing. Instead, now it's about allowing my individual soul to be a clear channel for Source to be expressed out in the world. What I have thought of as my own spiritual journey had, paradoxically, become my soul's pilgrimage through my human form." (George)

Our egos have been undergoing a transformative process since we first felt the stirrings of dissatisfaction with the limitations of an ego-centered life. This third threshold moves us beyond our separate and personal sense of self into a deeper identity with our souls and our Source. We expand beyond the personal awareness of the ego into a state of being in which our ego becomes of service to our Source instead of to itself. It is the natural result of the intentional choices we make to foster our authenticity.

"I was fired from my job yesterday. It came as a terrible shock. I thought I was doing everything I could do to make it work. My boss just told me, out of the blue, that it was just a misfit—that I wasn't suited to this job. And he proceeded to tell me all the ways I wasn't suited. Finally, I just stopped him and said, "I can't take anymore. I have to go home." I was devastated. Then I went to my spiritual director, and as I was related this story to her, I found myself telling all the ways that the job didn't suit me. In order to do this job, I've squelched all my creativity, my ability to speak out, and have just tried to fit myself into a job which I realize doesn't fit at all. At first, I wanted to fight my firing, but now, I see that my best choice is go to my boss tomorrow and say, "You're right. How much notice do you need?" It really

is so simple. . . when I'm in my authentic self, it is very
clear to me that I have to choose work that expresses
more fully who I am" (Stephanie)

It is true that as we continue to deepen into the mystery of
our Source, we have less control, fewer answers, and our old ways of
making things happen no longer work. We realize that we have fewer
doubts, questions, fears, and less need to know. We also have fewer
choices, because we are clearer about whom we are. We have no need
to spend time trying to discern where we are going or what we want
or need. Gradually and radically, we let go of these values of the ego
in a steady movement into a deeper trust in the goodness of our
own authenticity. We are learning to trust that being present in our
authenticity in all aspects of our lives is all that is necessary to bring
the wholeness inherent in our spiritual journey out into the world.

However, even though our egos are gradually aligning
with our spiritual source, they may continue to have a lingering
attachment to us being the best spiritual beings that we can
be. By giving us an image of some mold, or criteria, that we
are supposed to fit, our egos set conditions on us that still
hold us back from being fully spiritually present. For example,
we can still get caught in comparing ourselves to someone we
perceive as more spiritual than we are. Then, we run the risk
of being led off our own authentic path. Once again, we have
to release the ego's image of whom we are "supposed" to be,
but this time, we are fine-tuning a process we already know
how to do. We return to the open heart and we deepen our
attentiveness to what we hear there. It is the heart that is the
home of unconditional acceptance and trust of soul and source.

"I had an assignment from my spiritual group to
consider the question, 'What do I believe?' The following
week, I brought to the group a long list of my beliefs
ranging from a belief in a Source of loving energy, to a
belief that walking to work enhances my day. One of
my fellow group members read a list of very profound,

Why
Are there
So few in the court
Of a perfect saint?
Because
Every time you are
Near Him
You have to
Leave pieces
Of your
Ego
With
The hatcheck
Girl
Who won't give them
Back
O
O
O
U
C
H
Hafiz[2]

esoteric beliefs. I immediately compared my list to his, and thought mine were too mundane. Then, after some discussion, I realized that my ego was alive and well here, and that there was really no need to compare myself to anyone and, in the process, undermine my own authenticity." (Paula)

All of the inner work thus far, has required us to learn how to trust. First we learned to trust our egos to lead us into becoming a competent, confident self in the world. Then we learn to trust the deeper self that lies beyond the ego.—our soul and Spirit, God, or Source. Now, we know how to return to that deeper place where trust resides.

"I seem to go along well for awhile, then I get an attack of self-doubt. It shows up when I face a new challenge; speak out for what I believe in, or when I don't; or when I am overwhelmed. Self-doubt is so uncomfortable. I feel that whatever I do will not be the right thing, or that it won't be good enough. When this happens, feel so desperate that I turn to some kind of inspirational reading, and eventually I find myself centered once again, and trusting my Source." (Keith)

The third threshold we are moving across is not of our personal making. While this can be said of each threshold, our perception has been that we, personally, have done a lot of work to make them happen (staying conscious can be a lot of work). We are clearly aware that this third threshold is a spiritual state of being—a state of grace. We are simply aware one day, of having no more fear, of having no more questions—no more *need* to know, and the idea of being an "I" seems irrelevant. "I" doesn't define us anymore. While we function in the world as an "I," our real identity is no longer anchored in the "I" of the ego. Our identity has shifted so that now we are *aware* of becoming solidly anchored in soul and Source. Furthermore, we see that we have always been anchored here, we just weren't as aware of it as we are now.

"At a conference in which I was the leader, I had to confront a participant who was being asked to leave, and then work with the rest of the participants about his leaving. Ordinarily I would have been nervous about the confrontation, felt the need to have the 'right' words to say, and worried about how I would be perceived by the rest of the group.

I was surprised to find myself calm, assured and open to what might evolve. I had no fear, no questions, no awareness of 'me.' I was just present to the work ahead of me. Sometime later in the day, I stopped to take a breath, and realized with amazement that I was being carried by grace all day. I was filled with a deep sense of gratitude." (Suzanne)

"My partner has been very ill. For a year now, life has been a series of doctors visits, tests and treatments. Typically, I would have been fearful, anxious, self-protective, and wanting to control the process. Instead, I am so present in this situation, that there is no fear, no need to control anything, and no emotional upheaval, and no sense of 'I.' I am aware of this grace within me that keeps me present, through no effort of my own. What I feel is love and gratitude." (Sally)

It is in an odd place that we find ourselves. In earlier shifts, we had to make a conscious decision to go deeper, with it's accompanying emotional upheaval. Now, we simply find ourselves in this state, with no emotion about it at all. We merely are beings carried by grace with no emotional fanfare. In fact, this a spiritual shift that we do not experience emotionally—it is a purely spiritual occurrence. We can feel the freedom from fear and doubt—like having a greatly expanded ability to breathe. Inherent in the ground of this state of being is gratitude, compassion, and love.

"I have to remember that I am grounded in those qualities that I have spent my life seeking—love, trust,

Like dripping water wearing away a stone, our egos are transformed through our gradual identification with our souls and the Source from which everything comes.

compassion, and gratitude. I don't have to work to have them, I just have to remember that they are always flowing through me." (Sally)

How do we support ourselves in this state of being? One way is to embody what we are experiencing and learning. We continue to consciously attend to the way our body feels when we are being authentic, and free of fear. We find practices that foster that awareness, such as breathing deeply, laughing, yoga, dance, walking in the woods or on the beach, meditation, and other spiritual practices.

"When I am faithful to my daily practice of yoga, I find that I stay more stable in this place of no fear. The breathing and movement release any physical or emotional tension that might generate anxiety. The yoga brings me back to my self." (Joey)

"Bowing is my central practice. When I bow, I am consciously giving up my will and offering my will, my self, and my future time, up to God. I am uniting my Spirit with the Creator. I feel closest to god at that moment, and for that reason, will often bow mentally during the day. It is the great and unfailing connection. There is no revelation in this moment, no comfort—only simple silence and rest. It is said that we should bow, even in the last moment. I hope that I will be able to bow in my last moment. I place my hands together when I bow because I believe that when we put out hands together we are one in the oneness that goes beyond understanding. I am grateful that this practice was given to me." (Judi)

Another way to support ourselves is remembering where we were before this state of being. As we recall what has brought us here, we also remember our wisdom and that we can trust ourselves in our own particular process.

"Sometimes, when I am asked to give a sermon during a worship service, I get very nervous. Because I

don't do it on a regular basis, I begin to doubt my ability to do it. Then, as I begin planning the liturgy and writing the sermon, I remember that this is part of my 'call' and I also remember that I can trust myself to do this. I may still be physically nervous, but my soul is at peace." (Suzanne)

Storytelling is also a way to support this state of grace. We tell our stories of transformation to each other in order to claim the essence of them. Our storytelling helps to build a community of mutual support and allows our souls to celebrate their visibility and voice.

"I belong to a small group of women who gather regularly to share the stories of their soul's deepening awareness. I find it very helpful to have this regular opportunity to articulate each new awareness that I come to know. This is a safe place to bring the essence of my soul into the open and to give it a voice. When I tell my story out loud, it becomes more real and grounded in me. (Suzanne)

This state of grace, that we have begun to live in, subsumes and embraces the ego and, thereby, diminishes its power. However, until we are stable in this state, the ego will always come forth if we engage in any sort of self-aggrandizement. The ego loves to take credit for mystical experiences, and to make them its own. In reality, mystical experiences happen at a different level of consciousness than our ego. Our ego selves neither initiate nor control them. So, another way to support ourselves in this state of grace is to recognize how ordinary we are even in our spiritual understanding. As we gain stability in this state of grace, we become aware of the subtle nuances in life that can evoke the ego's appetites for external recognition.

Throughout this process of ego transformation, what has been expanding is our awareness of how much more we are than our egos. We are learning to turn our faces toward our souls, in the way a sunflower follows the sun.

"When I came to understand that there are mythic patterns in all our lives, I knew that all of us, often unbeknownst to ourselves, are engaged in a drama of soul which we were told was reserved for gods, heroes, and saints."

Deena Metzger[3]

SELF-REFLECTION

1. Write, paint, draw, make a collage, or sculpt an image of where you are in the process of the transformation of your ego. Sit with the image and meditate on it. When you are ready, share it with someone you think would understand.

"I" doesn't define us anymore. Our real identity is no longer anchored in the ego, but rather in the soul.

> *"One of my images of the transformation of my ego is the labyrinth. As I follow the labyrinth's path toward the center, I think I'm going to get there quickly. But in the pattern of the labyrinth the center is illusive. The path takes me far from the center and then brings me closer many times before I can actually enter the center. My ego seems to be on a similar journey—at times closer to my center, and at others farther away. Yet, all the while, my ego has been slowly losing the will to be a separate force". (Sally*

2. Recalling the stories of Suzanne, Joey, or Judi, in this chapter, what are the ways *you* support yourself when you feel you have lost your footing?

Notes

Pilgrimage of the Soul

Notes

12

THE SOUL'S PILGRIMAGE

The soul has as its purpose and mission the task of bridging the world of the eternal and the everyday world in which we live. Once it leads us out of the limitations of our lives as citizens of this world and allows us to spend some time as citizens of the kingdom within, it marches us back into our former world and tells us to help it to build the bridge.

Father Paul Keenan[1]

If we could go back over our journey from the perspective of this new state of being, with our egos largely transformed, what might it look like?

"In everything I do, I am aware that my soul is in motion. It is a paradox to me, that while I experience a profound interior silence and stillness, this stillness and silence is actually moving—the eternal dance of soul and source. All that has really changed throughout this whole evolution of myself is my perception--the stripping away of the veils set up by my ego, in my efforts to be fully human." Claudia

What if the ego is actually an expression of the soul, to be developed and transformed? One could say that the ego is a tool that enables the soul to develop a human being capable of navigating the material fabric of life on Earth. Perhaps we seem to "forget" our origins in Spirit because we can't see past our egos until some of the veils separating ego from soul are dissolved.

Self and the Soul

The earliest veil of separation laid down by our egos is the distinction between self and other. Our cultural conditioning taught us that everything other than ego, was outside us, including our souls and the sacred. This veil of separation has been gradually dissolving through our spiritual practices. At first we become present *to* the sacred, giving attention to that which stirs our souls. The idea is that the soul is at the very center of us, with all other aspects of us focusing on external relationships and activities. These aspects come from our ego and may be thought of as our various roles in life. Some of them may actually be trying to protect the soul from what they perceive as danger.

This protection works two ways. While the soul may be considered precious and in need of protection, these parts of our ego also fear the loss of their identity and power if the soul were to become the leader. So, they become gatekeepers, keeping the soul at bay. What they don't see with their limited vision, is that they are already an expression of the soul, no matter how distorted that expression may be.

Here is an example of what happened to Randy in spiritual direction:

Spiritual Director (SD): "Who is in charge of your life?"
Randy: "What I have is a part of me who is in charge of my daily life. This part tries to bring balance to my life by keeping the more outrageous parts of me in line

*(a stern grumpy old man—a naysayer to everything, a
lost boy who is afraid, and a crying baby who screams
so loudly that it shuts down my whole system.) The
'balancer' also protects my soul from being hurt or
damaged by these parts of me and by outside influences.
All of these parts of me are only vaguely aware of my
soul. The 'balancer' likes to meditate because it brings a
sense of peace."
SD: What if the 'balancer' were to get more acquainted
with your soul?"
Randy, "The idea of the 'balancer' getting to know my
soul is frightening to me because I'm afraid that I'll fall
in and disappear, and then all the rest of me would go
to hell.
SD: "Consider the idea that the 'balancer' may have a
limited view of the soul because of it's own agenda—
that of protecting the soul. In order for the balancer
to protect the soul, the soul has to be perceived as small
enough, and separate enough, for the balancer to protect.
But, what if the balancer is only seeing a portion of the
soul? What if, in fact, the balancer is imbedded in the
soul? What if the soul actually holds the 'balancer' and
all aspects of you?
Randy: "It would be like discovering a loving parent
that I didn't know I had."*

As we can allow the idea that all aspects of ourselves are
imbedded in the soul, we become more present *in* the sacred, and
we started living consciously from our souls. During the dissolution
of the veil of separation of self from soul, we become increasingly
aware of our unity with all life. We all share the same life force; yet
present a diversity of expression.

Belonging and the Soul

For most of our lives we have this human need to belong—to

someone, to some place, to some community, or to some vocation. Belonging is important to our developing egos. It gives us an identity and a context for who we are in relation to others, our geographical place on the earth, and a sense of purpose. Belonging seems to be a large part of life's quest. In fact, much of our spiritual journey is the desire and the effort to belong to our Source.

The experience that we call the dark night of the soul, and we can have more than one, is really about the suffering of the ego. It is the ego's realization of its separation from soul and source, and the realization of the ego that it is powerless to change that unless it relinquishes its will. Even though it is a deep suffering, it is not the soul that is suffering. It is as if the soul is working "behind the scenes" to heighten our awareness of separation, as well as the emotional and behavioral patterns that we have developed that uphold the will of the ego. How can the ego be transformed if we cannot see how it operates in our lives? Yet, while the dark night forces us to see how desperate we really are for soul connection, the soul is working to dissolve the veil of separation that is our human need to identify ourselves with that to which we belong. As this need dissolves, we realize that we *are* that to which we were yearning to belong. We are one with soul and Source. The soul just *is,* it doesn't have a need to belong.

"After my divorce, I lived alone for a couple of years. During that time, I often felt lonely—like had no place to belong. Gradually, I began to realize that I really wasn't unhappy in this solitary state. I had my own soul for company, and it was marvelous to discover all the ways in which my very own soul gave me a sense of belonging, of being at home without other people or familiar communities or places. I had time to listen to my own self and to find within me the choices and directions I now wanted to pursue.

Even after I found another partner and moved into her home, I didn't need her or her home to give me a sense of identity or belonging—I carried that within me". (Jeff)

Time and the soul

Another veil of separation that dissolves is our concept of time. As we saw earlier, we develop the concepts of past, present and future to give us a sense of continuity in our lives. It seems that we are always waiting for some future event. Waiting is also inherent in the spiritual journey. We wait in meditation, we wait for the dark nights to lift, we wait to hear the inner voice, and we wait for the next spiritual experience. From a human perspective we say that the soul has its own pace and time. This idea seems to help us to wait without so much angst. Yet, the ego in us will always wait for the next event.

From the soul's perspective the present moment is all there is, so whenever we're "waiting" we're still engaged to some extent with the ego. The soul doesn't "wait." Time belongs to Earth life.

Another veil of separation associated with our human concept of time is the distinction between life and death—existence and nothingness, and the intrinsic fear of death. What the soul has been teaching us is that life is continuous. It is only the human form, the body, that fails and dies. The soul lives on.

"When my father died, I was in deep grief for over a year. He had been a quiet, unconditionally loving man, who I had loved and always wanted to please. Some time during the second year after his death, I became aware of a presence with me, especially when I was concerned about one of my children, or in doubt about my own choices or future directions. I began to recognize this presence as my father's Spirit—not in a physical, ghostly way, but being in the company of a Spirit or soul of love, acceptance, and reassurance. Now, eleven

years after his death, I often find myself in thoughtful dialogue with him and receive from his Spirit support, encouragement, and a sense of love that lives on long after his physical death. This soul to soul communion also happens with my grandmother, and both are in some ways a deeper form of communication than I had with either my grandmother or my father when they were alive." (Suzanne)

Love and the soul

Over time, we sense a new foundation of solidity, strength, inner silence and stillness. We experience this state as love, a profound knowing that we are one with all life. An inherent aspect of love is the urge to express it in the world. Whether we are in silence and stillness, serving in a soup kitchen, working at our jobs, tending our children or grandchildren, the soul is actively expressing itself to the degree that we allow it to do so.

We allow the soul to move fully and without hindrance when we act out of this state of love, not out of a sense of obligation, self-judgment, or resentment. When we act out of obligation, self-judgment, or resentment, we build up a resistance to whatever we are doing. Just as if we were to put a resistor into an electrical current, we impede the flow of electricity, or redirect its flow. So, too, do we impede or misdirect the flow of our spiritual energy. Expressing love out in the world is not just a mental or emotional exercise, or a task to accomplish. It is not something we do to gain love and recognition. It is, no longer, an ego-driven movement. We do not *do* love—we *are* love.

The soul acts out of the love that is its nature. If we are embodying our souls, then we also embody love. Because we do embody love, it has to come through us in all that we do. Loving from the soul is expressing the soul's state of being. To fully embody love means that we must love ourselves, including this human form that we inhabit. Believing ourselves to be totally lovable just as we are, can be a huge shift for many of us. Those parts of us that continue to engage in self-judgment may still hold on to the belief that we are not "good enough" to be wholly lovable.

> *"Believing that I am lovable is very difficult*
> *for me. I grew up with the notion that one strives to*
> *be perfect, and anything less than perfection doesn't*
> *count. Loving oneself was considered to be selfish and*
> *narcissistic. I like the idea that I might be lovable,*
> *even though there is a strong part of me that judges me*
> *harshly for even entertaining that idea. But, I just keep*
> *asking myself the question, 'What if I really am lovable?'*
> *Perhaps as I persist with this question, it will take root*
> *inside." (Natasha)*

This can be one of the last veils of separation to dissolve. These parts are lovable simply because they, too, are aspects of this human/soul creation.

Beliefs and the Soul

One more veil that is stripped away is our need for the beliefs which we have used to identify ourselves and to give our lives meaning.

> *"I asked members of a spiritual group that I was*
> *leading to tell each other their beliefs, and how they live*
> *by them. As the stories were going around the circle,*
> *I realized that I no longer have any beliefs. Instead, I*
> *seem to have a profound certainty of knowing that my*
> *identity lies beyond whatever I might believe. It isn't*
> *that I can't list things that I believe in, it's just that they*
> *no longer tell me who I am." (Sally)*

The dissolution of the veils of separation from our Source is the soul's pilgrimage of coming out, through our human form, into the world. The soul's urge is toward full expression, carrying us into places of deep contemplation, joy, and connection, and to express this connection out into the world in the form of service and leadership. This passion comes out of this state of being, and is not to serve ourselves, but rather to serve the greater good. Our personal goal, then, becomes one of seeking out ways that will give this state of being adequate expression in service to others.

See Self-Reflection on following pages

SELF-REFLECTION

1. Draw a diagram similar to the one on the following page of the parts/aspects of you around your soul in the center.

> Who are the various parts of you? What roles do they play in your life?
>
> What are their good intentions?
>
> What are their extreme behaviors?
>
> Which part of you plays the most central role(s) in your life?
>
> Would you say that this part of you is mostly in charge of your life?
>
> Which parts of you do you like the best?
>
> Which parts of you do you dislike and wish they would just go away?
>
> Which parts are in alliances with each other.

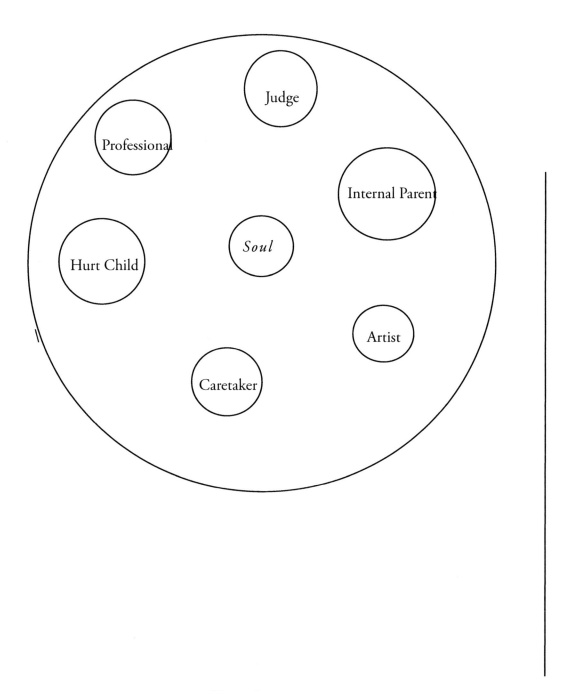

Figure 2

An example of a human personality with it's ego aspects before
spiritual integration.

2. Now draw a diagram similar to the next page with the soul surrounding and embracing all of your aspects/parts instead of being in the center of them.

> Which aspects of you resist the notion that they are, in fact, an aspect of the soul?
>
> What would those parts need in order to be willing to offer their skills and knowledge in service to the soul.

This second diagram illustrates how, as the ego is transformed, all our strengths, knowledge, and skills are available within the soul, and in service to the soul without the old ego boundaries.

Figure 3
An example of a human/spiritual being after integration
and transformation of the ego.

Pilgrimage of the Soul

Notes

Notes

Pilgrimage of the Soul

13

SERVICE and LEADERSHIP

> *"We are all capable of leading from our souls.*
> *We were made to do it that way in the first place. When*
> *we begin to lead from our souls, we are coming home,*
> *coming to the place in which we were meant to be, even*
> *though it usually means living counter to the culture.*
> *But inside, it is a wonderful and relieving feeling."*
> Janet Hagberg in *Real Power*

As our separations between ego and soul dissolve, a passion for service comes out of this integrated state of being. This urge is not to serve ourselves, but rather to serve the greater good. Our personal goal, then, becomes one of seeking out ways that will give this state of being adequate expression in service to others. Our personal discovery is that leadership and service really are yoked.

Leadership in this sense is often very quiet, in the background, gentle – certainly with no agenda of its own. It's offered one-on-one or in larger settings. It sometimes calls for the "leader' to be in the public eye and sometimes does not. It is never self-serving, but comes out of a deep place within us as a desire to be present in a way that will enable another to open to new awareness.

"Sometimes in my role as a leader, I am simply called to stand along side someone and offer affirmation and support a\s they begin to take hold of their own understanding of their personal work or of their leadership role." (Caryn)

"I'm a new dentist in a practice with a staff I inherited. Many of them come to work each morning complaining about the weather,
the old office politics, each other—you name it. This creates an environment of toxic energy that, literally, makes me ill. So, I decided to gather the group together each morning, and suggest that we each think about how we can make each day the best we can. It worked! Now we see who can come up with the best ideas. The energy of the office has changed drastically" (Tom)

This form of leadership anticipates transformation – both in those the leader is called to serve and in the leader herself. This "servant leader" lives a life of freedom and self-reflection – deeply aware of the daily path the soul opens before her. Each expression of servant leadership is unique to each person. Each soul leads in its own way.

"When I am preparing to lead a particular group in a spiritual experience, my internal preparations usually involve a lot of sitting in contemplation. I go below any anxiety or self-doubt I might have to a place in which I can focus on the needs of the group, and what it is that I would like to offer them. I consider the variety of ways I might approach the experience that I want them to have. The goal is always to find the best approach I can that will enhance their spiritual process, wherever in the journey they might be. I give as much time in contemplation as it takes for the inner knowledge to rise from my depths. What is also happening, at the same time, is my

willingness to trust the information that comes to me."
(Sally)

> *"The four phases of encouraging leadership in others runs like this for me:*
> - *I do it.*
> - *We do it together*
> - *You do it, and I support you*
> - *You do it, and I go on to do something else, releasing ownership of whatever that area of leadership was about." (Suzanne)*

In most societies many people are socialized or programmed to become either servants or leaders. Servant-leader is a paradox but not a contradiction. The opposite of leader is follower; opposite of servant is master. The word servant does not mean follower, the word leader does not mean master. A servant-leader is one who is dedicated to helping those who seek help. One who is just and caring. One who sees what needs to be done for those members of the community whom others ignore or belittle or mistreat – and insures that it is done. One who can be trusted and who has earned respect from a wide range of people – peers, superiors, those who have benefited from the person's actions.

> *"Because of my own experience as a victim of clergy misconduct, and through my own healing process, I have come to a place where I feel called to be an advocate on behalf of victims of similar abuse. Consequently, I have helped to organize, recruit and train other victim advocates. Together we work to impact the systems of the church which continue to favor the perpetrators and re-victimize the victims. Our group functions with great faithfulness, integrity, and a vision for justice on behalf of the victims we assist. Our efforts are slowly making a difference in the lives of individuals, affected congregations, and in the larger systems of the church." (Edith)*

Soulful living means being fully immersed in the day-to-day matters that make up our lives. It often amazes us to realize that the soul drives us back to our normal lives. While the soul maintains its focus on things that are eternal, it insists that we bring those internal verities to bear upon our daily world.

Fr. Paul Keenan [2]

To be a leader does not mean that we have "arrived," or that our spiritual journey is finished. Rather, we continue to live as authentically as possible in whatever state we find ourselves.

*"It was quite a surprise to me to find that I will
never 'arrive.' Yet, now, I revel in the freedom of the
constant change and growth of awareness. " (Sally)*

To live authentically without internal separations means that we accept the call to honor our oneness with soul, Source, and all life. We respond to this call by being of service to others. Service is no longer a choice, but a way of living. Our souls seem to require it.

*"I have come to a place where my deepest desire
is to live simply with gratitude for all that unfolds before
me each day. A recent breath prayer for me is:
May all I do, Holy One, further your work in
the world."(Suzanne)*

SELF REFLECTION

MEDITATION

Find a comfortable position to sit in, and take several slow, deep breaths to quiet yourself. When you feel centered, imagine holding the globe of the Earth in your hands. As you hold it, turn it slowly, noticing the oceans and continents. Let your attention be drawn to particular places on the Earth--

• places where you have lived, or have friends or loved ones.

• places you have traveled or feel drawn toward.

• places whose land or environment is in distress.

• places whose people may be struggling.

Offer a prayer of gratitude for this planet. Send healing energy from your hands for the highest good of Earth and the life it sustains. Send healing energy to those places on the Earth that are in need of healing and wholeness. Notice in what way you may be feeling called to be of service in the world.

Consider using this meditation as part of your spiritual practice.

174

Notes

REFERENCES

INTRODUCTION

[1]Loder, Ted, <u>Tracks in the Straw</u>, <u>Tales Spun from the Manger</u>, Innisfree Press, Inc. Philadelphia, PA,1985.

CHAPTER 1

[1]Harvey, Andrew, <u>The Direct Path</u>, Broadway Books, New York, 200.

[2]Singh, Kathleen Dowling, <u>The Grace in Dying, A Message of Hope, Comfort and Spiritual Transformation.</u> HarperSanFrancisco, 2000.

[3]Ibid.

[4]Rumi, "Don't Go Back to Sleep", <u>The Soul of Rumi,</u> Translations by Coleman Barks, HarperSanFrancisco, 2001.

CHAPTER 2

[1]Caplan, Mariana, <u>Halfway Up The Mountain</u>, Hohm Press, Prescott, Arizona, 1999.

[2]Aurobindo, Sri, <u>The Divine Life, Pondicherry, India, 1977.</u>

CHAPTER 3

[1]Romans, 8:26, <u>The Holy Bible, New Revised Standard Version</u>, Holman Bible Publishers, 1989.

[2]DeMello, Anthony, <u>One Minute Wisdom</u>, Doubleday, New York, 1986

[3]Singh, Kathleen Dowling, <u>The Grace in Dying, A Message of Hope, Comfort and Spiritual Transformation.</u> HarperSanFrancisco, 2000.

[4]Chittister, Joan, <u>Illuminated Life, Monastic Wisdom for Seekers of Light</u>, Orbis Books, Maryknoll, New York, 2000.

[5]Rilke, Ranier Maria, <u>Book of Hours: Love Poems to God,</u> Berkeley Publishing, New York, NY, 1996.

CHAPTER 4

[1]Rumi, in <u>The Soul of Rumi</u>, Translations by Coleman Barks, HarperSanFrancisco, 2001.

[2]Derricote, Toi, "Sitting with Myself in the Seton Hall Deli at 12 o'clock Thursday before I Read with the Great Poets at the Emily Dickinson Poetry Festival," in <u>Visiting Emily--Poems Inspired by the Life and Work of Emily Dickinson.</u> Edited by Sheila Coghill and Thom Tammaro, University of Iowa Press, 2000.

CHAPTER 5

[1]Appleton, George, *Journey into Wholeness, Vol 10, No. 3*

[3,]St. John of the Cross, <u>The Collected works of St. John of the Cross</u>, ICS Publications, Washington, DC 1991, bk 1.

[3]Singh, Kathleen Dowling, <u>The Grace in Dying, A Message of Hope, Comfort and Spiritual Transformation.</u> HarperSanFrancisco, 2000.

[4]St. John of the Cross, <u>The Collected works of St. John of the Cross</u>, ICS Publications, Washington, DC 1991, bk 1.

[5]McEntyre, Marilyn Chandler, "What to Do in the Darkness," in Weavings, March/April, 2004, Upper Room, Nashville, TN.

[5]Kidd, Sue Monk, <u>When the Heart Waits</u>, HarperSanFrancisco, 1990

CHAPTER 6

[1]Chittister, Joan, <u>Illuminated Life, Monastic Wisdom for Seekers of Light</u>, Orbis Books, Maryknoll, New York, 2000. Thoughts in Solitude, Farrar Straws & Giroux, New York, NY, 1956.

[3]Beattie, Melody, <u>Peace Prayers</u>, HarperSanFrancisco, 1992.

[4]DelBene, Ron, <u>The Breath of Life</u>, Upper Room Books, Nashville, Tennessee, 1992.

CHAPTER 7

[1]O'Murchu, Diarmuid, <u>Quantum Theology, Spiritual Implications of the New Physics</u>, The Crossroad Publishing Company, New York, 1998.

CHAPTER 8

[1]Cummings, Charles, No reference could be found.

[2]Sarton, May, Journal of a Solitude, W.W. Norton & Company, New York, 1973.

[3]Okri, Ben, in De Waal, Esther, "Attentiveness," In Weavings, A Journal of the Christian Spiritual Life, Vol. XVII, No. 4, Upper Room Ministries, Nashville, Tennessee, 2002.

[4]Lao-Tzu, from Tao Te Ching, translated by Stephen Mitchell, Harper Perennial, 1988.

[5]Thich Nhat Hanh, A Guide to Walking Meditation, Fellowship Publications, Nyack, New York, 1985.

CHAPTER 9

[1]Smith, Huston, Forgotten Truth, Harper & Row, New York, 1976.

[2]Caplan, Mariana, Halfway up the Mountain, Hohm Press, Prescott Arizona, 1999.

CHAPTER 10

[1]Saliers, Emily, Indigo Girls Recording, *Watershed*, from the album, Retrospective, Sony Music Entertainment Corp., 2000

[2]Linn, Dennis, et al., Sleeping with Bread, Holding What Gives you Life, Paulist Press, Mahwah, New York, 1995.

[3] Rupp, Joyce, Out of the Ordinary, Ave Maria Press, Notre Dame IN, 2000.

CHAPTER 11

[1]Singh, Kathleen Dowling, The Grace in Dying, A Message of Hope, Comfort and Spiritual Transformation. HarperSanFrancisco, 2000.

[2]Hafiz, The Gift, Penguin Compass, New NY, 1999.

[3]Metzger, Deena, "Miracle at Canyon de Chelly, "Stories of the Spirit, Stories of the Heart: Parables of the Spiritual Path from Around the World, edited by Christina Feldman and Jack Kornfield, Harper Collins, 1991.

CHAPTER 12

[1]Keenan, Father Paul, <u>Stages of the Soul: The Path of the Soulful Life,</u>
<u>Contemporary Books, Chicago, 2000.</u>

CHAPTER 13

Hagberg, Janet, <u>Real Power, Stages of Personal Power in Organizations,</u>
Sheffield Publishing Company, Salem, WI, 2002.
[2]Keenan, Father Paul, <u>Stages of the Soul: The Path of the Soulful Life,</u>
Contemporary Books, Chicago, 2000.

To order by mail:

Spirit Called My Name

or *Pilgrimage of the Soul*

please complete the following information:

Name_____

Address_____

City, State, Zip_____

_____copies of *Spirit Called My Name* @ $11.95

       per book.. . . . .   _____

_____copies of *Pilgrimage of the Soul* @ $17.00

       per book. . . . .   _____

Postage & handling for 1-4 copies $3.50

Washington residents add 8.1%   _____

       Total Amount Enclosed   _____

Make checks payable to Soaring Eagle Publishing

Mail to:

       Soaring Eagle Publishing

       PO Box 578

       Freeland, WA 98249

Or order by phone: 360-331-4412

       by fax: 360-331-4523

       by email: oneilcas@whidbey.com